# BORROMINI

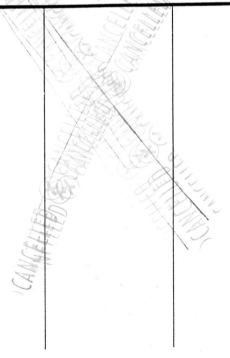

ANTHONY BLUNT

# BORROMINI

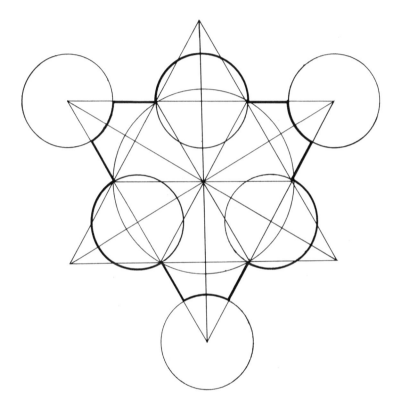

THE BELKNAP PRESS OF
HARVARD UNIVERSITY PRESS
CAMBRIDGE, MASSACHUSETTS
LONDON, ENGLAND

Library of Congress Cataloging in Publication Data

Blunt, Anthony, Sir, 1907–
  Borromini.

  Bibliography: p.
  Includes index.
  1. Borromini, Francesco, 1599-1667.
  2. Architects—Italy—Biography.
  3. Architecture, Baroque—Italy.
  NA1123.B6B56  720'.92'4  78-11320
ISBN 0-674-07925-6 (cloth)
ISBN 0-674-07926-4 (paper)

Designed by Gerald Cinamon

*To Charles and Barbara Robertson,*
*the creators of the Courtauld Summer Schools*

# Foreword

I first looked at the buildings of Borromini when I spent three months at the British School at Rome in the autumn of 1933. During that time I visited most of the Baroque churches of Rome in the company of Ellis Waterhouse – then librarian of the School – who was preparing his work on Roman painting of the same period.

I had approached Borromini and Roman Baroque as a whole from the wrong end. I had been fascinated for some years – in fact since I was a schoolboy when I was introduced to it by my elder brother Wilfrid – by the Baroque of Bavaria and Austria, and had visited most of the churches and palaces of those areas slowly but enjoyably by train, on a bicycle and on foot; and I came to Rome thinking that I ought, rather as a matter of duty than of pleasure, to study the roots of the style in Italy. What I saw in Rome was a revelation to me, and, though I have never given up my love for Johann Michael Fischer and Balthasar Neumann, my perspective was changed.

Ellis Waterhouse and I not only visited – and he and Colin Hardie, who was Director of the School, photographed – the great buildings of Borromini, Bernini and Pietro da Cortona – still relatively unknown to English students – but we also explored certain by-ways, such as the churches of the early eighteenth century by architects such as Carlo De Dominicis and Pietro Passalacqua; but from an early stage Borromini became for me the irresistibly great master, the one architect whose works were so subtle that one could go on examining and dissecting them, constantly discovering new beauties, new refinements, new ingenuities, and always in the end coming to the conclusion that what seemed at first sight to be freaks of fantasy were in fact variations based on an almost ruthlessly logical method.

I was however distracted by other preoccupations – mainly with Poussin and French seventeenth-century art – from pursuing my interest in Baroque architecture, and it was not till after the war that I came back to it. Even then I was again distracted from Borromini by my interest in Neapolitan and Sicilian Baroque; and I was also deterred from writing about him by my awareness of the fact that so much research was being carried out on him that it was an inappropriate moment to attempt any kind of synthesis. But once Borromini has bitten you he never lets go, and after much hesitation I decided to attempt to write a short book on him, in the hope of conveying to English-speaking readers something of his essential greatness. It was in this mood that I accepted the offer of John Fleming and Hugh Honour to write this book for the Penguin series 'The Architect and Society'. It must be emphasized, however, that I make no claim to add to our factual knowledge of Borromini's life or works. I have not discovered a single new document and if I have added a few items to the corpus of his drawings they are not of great importance. What I have aimed at is writing an account of his life and an analysis of his works in relatively intelligible language. I say *relatively* because Borromini seems to inspire those who write about him to do so in the most complicated and alembicated style, so that one tends to lose sight of the genuine and fascinating complexities of his art in the process of unravelling the complexities of the writer's style. I hope – and this hope may be vain – that I have avoided this pitfall as far as possible.

Many of the ideas in this book have been developed in the course of teaching and lecturing at the Courtauld Institute over the last thirty years and in many cases discussion with students has led me to see the problems involved more clearly. I cannot possibly name them all or specify their contributions but I wish to acknowledge my debt to them.

I also want to record my thanks to the photographic team of the Courtauld Institute, particularly to Constance Hill, their organizer, and James Austen, their photographer, for the superb photographs of Roman Baroque buildings which they made at my request, particularly of those by Borromini. Some of these were taken in 1974 but the most systematic campaign was carried out during the Courtauld Summer School organized in 1976 by Charles and Barbara Robertson, to whom I must record my deepest gratitude. Finally I must thank Elsa Scheerer who has patiently typed and retyped the text in I don't know how many versions and has prepared the index to the book.

When I was preparing the first draft of this book I had the luck to meet Dr Joseph Connors of Harvard University, who was carrying out research on Borromini for a Ph.D. at Princeton. He kindly read the text and made many useful suggestions and corrections, and in addition called my attention to a number of points which had escaped me. I hope that in due course his work on the Oratorio di S. Filippo Neri, of which a small part has been printed in an article in *Oratorium*, will be published in full, and in the meantime I want to record my great gratitude to him.

# Birth and Early Training

From his own day till the end of the nineteenth century Borromini was vilified as the great anarchist of architecture, the man who overthrew all the laws of the Ancients and replaced them with disorder, and who corrupted the taste of many architects in Italy and Central Europe for generations. Now students of architecture are more inclined to agree with the few almost fanatical admirers who supported him during his lifetime, and he is generally acknowledged as one of the greatest geniuses – perhaps the greatest – of Baroque architecture. In addition it is gradually being realized that, far from being an anarchist, he worked within rules as strict as those of his so-called classical rivals, and that his style was derived in great part from the study of those ancient builders whose principles he was accused of denying. Furthermore he was a neurotic and unhappy man, constantly dogged by disaster, often largely of his own creating, quarrelling even with his best patrons and closest friends. The same tension dominated his activity as an artist and he only reached the final solution to his problems by an almost maniacal concentration, which we can to some extent watch in the drawings he made when working out his designs.

Francesco Castello was born at Bissone on Lake Lugano in 1599. Later, after he had established himself in Rome, he called himself Borromini, which was a name used in his mother's family, but which may have had for the architect the added significance of recalling the name of the Borromeo family which had lately given to the world the great St Charles and his distinguished nephew Cardinal Federico. Borromini came of a family of stonemasons and was related to Domenico Fontana and Maderno, both of whom had moved to Rome, where they had established themselves as the most successful papal architects of the last decades of the sixteenth and the first of the seventeenth centuries, working for Sixtus V (1585–90) and for Paul V (1605–21) respectively.

At a very early age – one biographer says at nine, another at fifteen – Borromini went to Milan, the nearest major artistic centre, and

spent some years there before moving south to Rome, where he
arrived late in 1619. Milan was at this time the scene of great activity
in both the ecclesiastical and the artistic fields. Carlo Borromeo had
instituted a great movement of religious reform which was continued
by Federico and the effects of which were still being felt in the years
when Borromini was in the city. One of the Cardinal's principal
interests was in church building, on which he wrote a short treatise
to demonstrate how the decrees and the spirit of the Council of
Trent could be applied to such work, and Borromini was certainly
influenced by the buildings which had been recently erected or were
actually under construction. The most important architect of the
older generation, the Bolognese Pellegrino Pellegrini, called Tibaldi

1 and 2. Pellegrino Pellegrini Tibaldi:
*left*, S. Fedele, Milan, begun 1569; *right*, Collegio Borromeo, Pavia, begun 1564

3 and 4. Francesco Maria Ricchino:
*left*, S. Giuseppe, Milan, begun 1607; *right*, Collegio Elvetico, Milan, façade, begun 1627

(1527–96), who spent the years 1564 to 1585 in Milan, had evolved a variant of Michelangelo's style which was manifested in the sophisticated façade of the church of S. Fedele [1] and the monumental grandeur of the Collegio Borromeo in near-by Pavia [2]. Francesco Maria Ricchino (1583–1658) was only just beginning his career as an architect, but in the church of S. Giuseppe [3], begun in 1607, he was experimenting with new ideas which led directly to the Baroque. Later he was to take a crucial step towards the full Baroque in giving a deep curve to the façade of the Collegio Elvetico in Milan [4].

Milanese architects were, however, above all directing their energies towards the completion of the cathedral by the addition of a façade and the construction of the octagonal dome-tower over the crossing, called by the Milanese the Tiburio. Borromini may have arrived just in time to witness the last years of the active phase of building which went on from 1603 to 1610, but even if he did not he would certainly have seen the work that had been carried out and probably the designs which had been produced by the various architects involved in the completion of the building, who included Tibaldi and Ricchino. In this way he would have had the opportunity of seeing – and possibly even of working in – a mason's yard in which he would have been able to learn from the great Lombard tradition of construction and stone-cutting in which his own family had been trained. His mature work shows how much he learned from this experience.

He reached Rome at the end of a period of some decades during which Roman architecture had been almost dormant. Since the death of Michelangelo in 1564 the dominant influence had been Vignola, whose Gesù, begun in 1568, had set a pattern for the planning of Counter-Reformation churches and whose precise, almost dry, style, as shown for instance in the loggia of the Villa Giulia, had dominated the taste of his successors Giacomo della Porta [5] and Domenico Fontana, the two most successful Roman architects in the last decades of the sixteenth century. The only architect to understand the revolutionary discoveries incorporated in Michelangelo's last works, the Porta Pia [6] and the Sforza Chapel [7], was Giacomo del Duca [8], who in some ways acted as a sort of intermediary between Michelangelo and Borromini.

When Borromini reached Rome, however, it was as a decorative sculptor rather than as a stonemason or a builder that he first obtained work. He was taken in by a relative, Leone Garovo (or Garvo), who was engaged in the decoration of the portico of St

5. Giacomo della Porta: S. Maria dei Monti, Rome, 1580–81

6. Michelangelo: Porta Pia, Rome

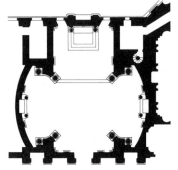

7. Michelangelo: S. Maria Maggiore, Rome, Sforza Chapel, plan

8 (*right*). S. Maria di Loreto, Rome, begun by Antonio da Sangallo, the Younger, 1502, dome by Giacomo del Duca, 1573–7

Peter's under Maderno and took on the boy as an assistant. He was thus immediately introduced to the workshop of the most important building project being undertaken in Rome at the time, the completion of St Peter's, and was brought into contact with Maderno, for whom he worked till the older architect's death in 1629 and through whom he established his reputation, first as a decorative sculptor and then as an architect. In the first capacity he is recorded in the early 1620s as employed by Maderno on St Peter's – where he was responsible for several marble cherubs' heads, including that over the Porta Santa in the portico [9] – as well as at other churches

9. Borromini: St Peter's, Rome, putto above Porta Santa, 1619–20

such as S. Andrea della Valle, on which Maderno was working. At St Peter's he was engaged in ironwork, and the wrought-iron gates to the Cappella del SS. Sacramento [10] are from his designs. The most remarkable work of sculpture with which he was connected at this time is the Fontana delle Api in the Vatican, a fantastic imitation of a rare type of ancient Roman fountain in the form of a mountain, in which the water is spouted by five bees, the heraldic symbol of Urban VIII (Barberini), who had been elected pope in 1623. Borromini is documented as having carved the fountain in 1626, but it is not certain whether he made the design for it, and it has also been attributed – not very plausibly – to Bernini.

In the same years he developed his astonishing ability as an architectural draughtsman with such success that he became Maderno's most important assistant and very soon was entrusted with more than the mere making of fair copies of his master's projects. Maderno, who was old and in bad health, began to allow him to design details himself and probably even to make contributions to his plans. In 1623, as a culmination to this development, he was allowed by Maderno to design the lantern on the dome of S. Andrea

10. Borromini: St Peter's, Rome, grille of Cappella del SS. Sacramento, 1627

della Valle. In the last years of Maderno's life Borromini was responsible for directing the work on the major commission on which he was engaged, the building of the Palazzo Barberini [11] for the newly elected pope, and here also he made positive contributions, certainly in details and possibly in the general planning. In 1637, eight years after Maderno's death, Borromini was called in to complete the decoration of the church of S. Lucia in Selci, which Maderno had rebuilt between 1605 and 1619. His work there shows very clearly what he learnt under his master at St Peter's, and the chapel which he designed for the church is decorated in the delicate style of stucco which was current in Rome under Pope

11. Carlo Maderno, Borromini and Bernini: Palazzo Barberini, Rome, west façade, 1629–33

Paul V and of which the portico of St Peter's can show some of the finest examples; but Borromini's decoration also shows a few personal touches, such as the cornice in which the eggs of the egg-and-tongue motif are replaced by cherubs' heads, a trick which he was to use many years later on the outside of S. Ivo della Sapienza [12].

Till the end of his life Borromini continued to have a deep respect and affection for his first master, to the point of asking in his will that he should be buried beside him. This was no doubt partly inspired by the fact that Maderno had been generous in allowing him a free hand and in encouraging his genius, but it may also be partly due to a desire on Borromini's part to emphasize the difference between Maderno and the artist under whom he found himself working on the death of the older master, Gian Lorenzo Bernini.

Borromini first came into contact with Bernini in 1624, when the latter was commissioned by Urban VIII to undertake the decoration of the crossing at St Peter's and the construction of the Baldacchino, and he was also his subordinate when Bernini took over the construction of the Palazzo Barberini, which was only just begun when Maderno died. Bernini, who was only twenty-six when he was called

12. Borromini: S. Ivo della Sapienza, Rome, cornice below dome

in to work on St Peter's, had made a sensational start as a sculptor, a field in which he showed unparalleled virtuosity and inventiveness, but he had had no training or experience as an architect, and he undoubtedly relied on Borromini's talent and technical skill to solve the many structural problems which arose in both commissions. In fact there is almost certainly substance in Borromini's accusation, made later in life after he had finally quarrelled with Bernini, that the latter exploited him and took the credit for his inventions.

The contrast between the two men was so great that they could hardly have avoided quarrelling. Bernini was brilliant and precocious, charming, sociable and tactful, moving easily in the papal court and captivating even the most arrogant of Louis XIV's courtiers on his visit to Paris in 1665. With the exception of a short period after the death of Urban VIII, when he was out of favour with his successor, Innocent X, his career was one of uniformly increasing success. In the arts his talent was universal. He was architect, sculptor and painter; he wrote poems and produced plays, writing the text and designing the settings and dresses; and his gifts were for the type of grand, somewhat theatrical style of architecture and decoration which was required at this stage of the Catholic Revival.

Borromini, though physically of a fine presence, lacked all the social graces. He was melancholy, nervous and uncompromising, and these qualities soon turned to a neurotic fear of all human contacts and a suspicion of people, which almost reached the stage of persecution mania. He quarrelled with many of his patrons and on several occasions threw up commissions, sometimes voluntarily, sometimes because he was threatened with dismissal. On one occasion in 1649 he caused his workmen to beat up a man whom he found tampering with the stonework of St John Lateran, to such effect that the man died, and it was only owing to the intervention of the pope that the architect was saved from severe punishment. Perhaps partly as a result of his early experiences with Bernini, he was so frightened that other architects would steal his ideas that just before his death he destroyed a great part of his unexecuted designs. It can have been no surprise to his few friends when he finally took his own life. But this intensely strained and nervous side of his character was accompanied by a passionate and total devotion to his art. He cared nothing for the things of the world and, according to his early biographers, often refused to take money in order to keep complete freedom in directing the buildings of which he was in charge. This obsession with his art is reminiscent of his contemporary, the painter Nicolas Poussin, who likewise gave up all the advantages which he could have gained in the public life of Rome in order to devote himself to his painting; but his problem was easier. He could shut himself up in his studio and refuse to see intruders; Borromini had of necessity to deal with patrons and workmen and to cope with practical problems. Perhaps it was for this reason that Poussin retained his sanity, whereas Borromini's mind became unsettled towards the end of his life.

But in all other respects the methods of the two artists were opposed. Poussin went from the elaborate to the simple, starting from a composition rich in figures, movements and incidents and gradually whittling away the inessentials till he reached the clearest and simplest statement of his theme. Borromini began with a simple plan and gradually elaborated it by introducing variations, replacing straight lines with curves, and then making those curves more complex till the final refinement of movement and space was attained. We can trace his steps along this path in his designs for S. Carlo and the Palazzo Carpegna (see below, pp. 58 and 162), and we can be fairly sure that in cases where the early stages of the design are not recorded he followed the same process of thought.

The contrast between Bernini and Borromini appears clearly if we examine the patrons for whom they worked. Bernini began as the infant prodigy discovered by Cardinal Scipione Borghese, nephew of Pope Paul V. Soon after the the election of Urban VIII in 1623 he was commissioned with the decoration of the crossing of St Peter's, the building of the Palazzo Barberini, the designing of Urban's tomb and other important papal works, and his favour continued unabated till the pope's death in 1644.

During this pontificate Borromini received a single public appointment, and that not directly from the pope: he was made architect to the university of the Sapienza, a post which enabled him to build one of his masterpieces, the church of S. Ivo. For the most part, however, he worked for religious orders, including the Oratorians, to whom he was introduced by a learned priest, Virgilio Spada. Spada was to help him more than any other patron in his career, for, when Urban VIII died in 1644, Spada became artistic adviser to his successor, Innocent X (Pamphili). Innocent was determined to reverse the policy of his predecessor in all fields, including the arts, and as a result Bernini found himself pushed aside, and Spada was able to bring his favourite to the notice of the pope. Through his agency Borromini received what was from the public point of view the most important commission of his career, to restore and remodel the interior of St John Lateran. At about the same time he was made Architect of the College of Propaganda Fide, a post which Bernini had previously held. However, within a few years Bernini gradually recaptured the favour of the pope, partly because of Borromini's constitutional inability to play the courtier, and, with the election of Alexander VII (Chigi) in 1655, he was fully reinstated; he became even more completely dictator of the arts than he had been under Urban VIII and was able to work on an even grander scale. The greatest monuments of the pontificate of Alexander – the Colonnade in front of St Peter's, the Cathedra Petri and the tomb of the pope within the church, the Scala Regia in the Vatican, and the two churches at Ariccia and Castel Gandolfo – were all papal commissions and all given to Bernini, who was also responsible for the church of the Jesuit Noviciate, S. Andrea al Quirinale. Borromini was allowed to complete the works that he had in hand – S. Ivo, Propaganda Fide and the Lateran – but he never received any major commissions from Alexander.

This neglect undoubtedly embittered him, but he must in fact have been happier working for the modest patrons by whom he was mainly employed than he would have been if he had been engaged on the great papal commissions. His first independent work, the church and monastery of S. Carlo alle Quattro Fontane, was built for an impoverished Spanish Order of Trinitarians; at S. Lucia in Selci and S. Maria dei Sette Dolori he was employed by the austere Augustinian nuns; the dome and campanile of S. Andrea delle Fratte were designed for the Minims, an order devoted to works of charity; the designs for the church of S. Giovanni di Dio or S. Giovanni Calabita (never executed) were made for the Padri Benefratelli who ran a hospital on the Isola Teverina, and the Oratory was built for the order founded by St Philip Neri, which strictly followed his rules of piety and simplicity. Patrons such as these were well satisfied by Borromini's approach to architecture, which – despite the originality and complexity of his buildings – was both practical and economical.

The private patrons who commissioned him to build palaces or villas were distinguished but they were the Spada, the Carpegna, the Falconieri, the Giustiniani, the del Bufalo and not – with the exception, for a short time, of the Pamphili – the much richer and more powerful papal families. Further, the commissions which he received from these patrons were usually of slight importance and often did not materialize.

Both Borromini and Bernini lived at the moment when the Baroque was being born in Rome, as the expression of the new feeling of optimism and aggressiveness in the Roman Catholic Church after the austere years of the Counter-Reformation, and both contributed to the invention of the new style in architecture – indeed with Pietro da Cortona they could be said to have created it – but their contributions could hardly have been more different. Bernini used the weapons of scale, dramatic light effects, the fusion of the three arts of painting, sculpture and architecture into a single whole, dramatic extension of the action across the whole space of a church, and the use of rich materials, coloured marbles and gilding; but his architectural forms were simple, sometimes even mean. Borromini worked on a small scale, usually in brick and stucco, but sometimes in travertine; he never used colour, and all the interiors of his churches are painted white; if he introduces sculpture, it is incorporated in the decoration of the building; and the light is used to emphasize the space, not to create dramatic contrasts. He attains his effects by purely architectural means, and in devising these he showed the utmost inventiveness. His spaces flow into one another; walls are curved or articulated in depth by columns and niches; he uses novel forms of arches, sometimes twisting them in three dimensions, and he invents fantastic forms for his domes, belfries and lanterns. The result is an architecture in which the essentially Baroque feature of movement is given its most brilliant expression, undisturbed by the distractions of colour, richness of materials or drama. One looks at Bernini's buildings with the eyes; one feels Borromini's with the whole body.

It is not at all easy to distinguish the share of Borromini in the buildings with which he was concerned while working under Maderno and Bernini. He is documented as having designed the lantern of Maderno's dome on S. Andrea della Valle, which already shows his ability to invent new and highly unconventional ideas, for in it the pairs of Ionic columns share a common capital, which spreads right across them, leaving room for a cherub's head between the two volutes. The problems connected with the Palazzo Barberini are much more complicated. Maderno was already old and ill when Pope Urban VIII began the planning of the palace in 1625, and though many features of the building are typical of his style as it is shown in his earlier palaces, such as the Palazzo Mattei di Giove, Borromini was certainly responsible for the oval spiral staircase in the right wing, which is a variant of Mascarino's staircase in the Quirinal. In one of the preliminary drawings the steps are shaped in very elongated S-curves, a form which Borromini was frequently to use later, but the architect abandoned this idea and, as built, the steps are straight. Borromini was also responsible for some of the particularly revolutionary details. Of these the most remarkable are the windows opening on the top floor of the loggia on the west front, which are set in false perspective arches, and the two in the bay flanking the loggia, which foreshadow many features of Borromini's later designs [18].

   With Bernini, who took over in 1629, his relations were more complex. The six smaller doors in the *salone* of the palace are basically from Borromini's design and most of the existing drawings for them are by him, but the introduction of sculpture in the form of busts in niches enclosed in the pediments suggests that Bernini had a hand in the completion of the designs. Borromini must also have played an important part in the execution of the central pavilion of the garden front, in which the brickwork is of a delicacy only paralleled in his façade of the Oratory of S. Filippo Neri, built a few years later.

Even more controversial is the question of the Baldacchino in St Peter's. The invention of the whole must certainly be credited to Bernini, though he incorporated in his design many features which had been suggested by the architects of earlier popes; but all the surviving drawings for the columns and entablature [13] are from

13. Borromini: Drawing for entablature of Baldacchino in St Peter's, Rome, 1624–7

the hand of Borromini. We have unhappily no means of judging how far he was following the dictates of his master and how far he was expressing his own ideas. Stylistically the Baldacchino is far closer to Bernini than to Borromini, but many of the details must be credited to the latter.

# Sources and Theories

There is very little written evidence to enlighten us on the subject of Borromini's ideas about his art, but a few documents survive which, while not actually composed by him, certainly reflect his ideas closely. The most important is the long introduction to the *Opus architectonicum*, with engravings of the Oratory of S. Filippo Neri, on which the architect was at work from 1637 to 1650. It is written in the first person, but the text was actually prepared by Virgilio Spada, who was Prior (*Preposito*) of the Oratory when Borromini worked on it. The manuscript was written during the architect's lifetime – Spada predeceased him – and he must have approved it. Another account of the building, written by Spada under his own name, exists and is of interest as reflecting Borromini's methods, though in this version Spada takes a great deal of the credit to himself.

The second source is a memorandum directed to Cardinal Camillo Pamphili, containing a project for the villa which the Cardinal was planning to build outside the Porta San Pancrazio. The document and the drawings attached to it are among Spada's papers in the Vatican Library and their connection with Borromini has been challenged, but whether or not either the drawings or the memorandum are actually from Borromini's own hand, it seems fairly certain that they expressed ideas with which he sympathized.

The last source is of a different kind. It is a manuscript guidebook to Rome composed by Fioravante Martinelli, a personal friend of Borromini, who championed his cause against those who supported Bernini and accused Borromini of being licentious in his treatment of architecture. As with the Spada documents we can be confident that the ideas expressed by Martinelli are in conformity with Borromini's own views because the two men were certainly very close friends and Martinelli submitted his manuscript to Borromini, who made a number of comments in the margin. These are corrections of factual details rather than expressions of personal views or theories, but obviously the architect would not have let pass any opinion with which he actually disagreed.

From these texts one fundamental point emerges immediately: that Borromini was a conscious innovator but that, like many other innovators, he relied much on the authority of previous masters in his art. This comes out very clearly in a sentence in the address at the beginning of the *Opus architectonicum* in which the architect says that his intention is to produce 'new things' and not 'conventional designs' but justifies his intention by referring to Michelangelo, who did likewise, and quoting his remark that 'one who follows others never gets ahead of them'. Borromini adds that he realizes he will not gain recognition easily for his inventions, because even Michelangelo was censured for his innovations in the architecture of St Peter's.

Martinelli makes the same point, but with reference to the Ancients instead of Michelangelo, when he says that Borromini was chosen to restore the church of St John Lateran 'for the liveliness of his invention [*la vivezza del ingegno*], for his knowledge of the rules of Vitruvius, and for his experience in imitating the works of the best masters of architecture among the ancient Greeks and Romans'; and he develops the point more fully in a long passage in which he defends Borromini against a critic, Filippo Maria Bonini, who, he says, wishes to make him out an architect

who works from caprice, who abhors the rules laid down by our predecessors, and the imitation of the Ancients, and who wants to introduce a new manner and new rules of building and to set up a school on these principles, [whereas in truth] the skill of the Cavaliere Borromini and his knowledge of all the sciences necessary to the architect are so abundant in him that, working like a true architect and making variations on the established rules, he has no pretensions to teach, but simply to clarify his own view on the work in hand. And if someone does not recognize his talent, it is necessary, in order to do so, to read Vitruvius and the other teachers and to have studied and worked in the profession from childhood.

He goes on to quote the names of real authorities who have praised the architect and ends by saying that in view of these opinions it is safe to conclude that in his works Borromini has 'without exception reached the supreme sanctuary of architecture [*summum templum Architecturae*]'. In another passage he returns to Bonini's accusation and turns the argument round against the critic, saying that 'the works of this rare *virtuoso* could serve as a new school' for architects.

From these and other passages it is clear that Borromini regarded Michelangelo and the Ancients as the two authorities to whom he could appeal with absolute confidence, and in fact many of his most revolutionary inventions are directly based on models drawn from them. It will therefore be necessary to examine his relation to them in some detail.

In the *Opus* Borromini frequently appeals to Michelangelo in connection with the Oratory of S. Filippo Neri. In the cloister there, for instance, he used giant pilasters linking the two superimposed arcaded loggias, and in justifying this argument he refers to the fact that Michelangelo had used such giant pilasters in his palaces on the Capitol, but that no one had used them since – a remark which shows that either he was unaware of the fact that Palladio had used such an order or that he was thinking only of Roman architects, or possibly that he preferred to ignore the case of Palladio in order to establish his own originality in reviving this feature.

The sight of Tibaldi's buildings in Lombardy, such as the church of S. Fedele in Milan or the Collegio Borromeo in Pavia, would have given Borromini a foretaste of Michelangelo's style, but only in a watered-down and academic form, and this experience would not have reduced the shock of seeing the originals which, as we know from his early biographers, he studied with passionate care. He was not the only architect in Rome at the time to study Michelangelo – indeed it had become an almost inescapable part of any architect's training – but not all architects drew the same lessons from the master. Michelangelo's most successful followers, Vignola and Giacomo della Porta, used motifs from his buildings but translated them into an academic idiom which made them widely acceptable but tame. As has already been said, only Giacomo del Duca, who had collaborated with Michelangelo in some of his last works, including the Porta Pia, had understood the really revolutionary elements in his latest style, and it is not by chance that there is in the Albertina (Rome 141)* a careful drawing of the façade of del Duca's S. Maria in Trivio by Borromini or a member of his studio, on which are recorded the exact measurements to the highest point that the draughtsman could reach with a ladder.

* The Albertina is the Austrian State collection of drawings, located in Vienna. It contains by far the largest group of drawings by Borromini, bought in the eighteenth century from Baron Stosch, who had acquired them from the heirs of the architect. Most of Borromini's drawings are kept in a single series; where mention is made in this book to the Albertina, followed by a number, it is this series we are referring to. A few of Borromini's drawings are, however, still in the Roman section of the topographically arranged drawings, and these we refer to as 'Rome ...'.

In the next generation Maderno, in completing St Peter's, had of necessity adopted motifs from Michelangelo, particularly in the treatment of windows, but like his academic predecessors he played safe, and where he had to continue a feature of Michelangelo's design for the exterior of the church along his nave or his façade he invariably softened and weakened it.

Borromini's approach is fundamentally different. Although he occasionally uses a feature from Michelangelo almost without variation – for instance the curious motif of the volute of an Ionic capital supporting a ball on the Porta Pia, which he puts around the cupola of S. Ivo [79] – his real interest was directed towards more fundamental principles of design, and when he had grasped Michelangelo's methods he adapted them freely to his own purposes.

He must have devoted intense study to the Cappella Sforza [7] and he learnt several different things from it. In the chapel Michelangelo had broken with the principle fundamental to Renaissance architecture of making each space in a building separate and complete, for the plans of the two side members – one can hardly call them chapels – are enclosed in shallow arcs which are far short of semi-circles, so that the spaces are incomplete and lead into the central domed area. Borromini uses this method in many of his buildings and throughout his career, but never more clearly than in his first independent commission, the church of S. Carlo alle Quattro Fontane [38], where the central space is flanked by two shallow bays, but he combines this Michelangelesque theme with another derived from the tradition of Peruzzi and Vignola, for his spaces are oval and not circular.

Borromini was, however, equally interested by another revolutionary feature of the chapel, the placing of the pairs of columns at the four corners of the central space, which, instead of being on the two main axes of the chapel, are set at an angle of 135°, so that one of them appears to thrust out into the central space. Borromini does not seem to have used this device in any of his church designs, but he adapts it to an almost sculptural idiom in the tomb of Cardinal Caracciolo in the Lateran [14] and in the central window of the Collegio di Propaganda Fide [140].

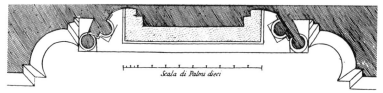

Scala di Palmi dieci

14. Borromini: S. Giovanni in Laterano, Rome, tomb of Cardinal Bernardo Caracciolo, after 1655, engraving

Borromini learnt almost as much from St Peter's as from the Cappella Sforza; he derived more, however, from the decorative motifs than from the general plan because, except at St John Lateran, where he was tied by the existing buildings, he never worked on a scale which allowed him to use Michelangelo's gigantic inventions in the treatment of space. In the entablature of the lower order on the façade of the Oratory he uses mouldings with a sloping corona and a curved frieze, like those on the Palazzo dei Conservatori, but he seems to have been particularly fascinated by the windows in the attic [15a and b]. He took the slanting consoles with guttae which

15a and b. Michelangelo: St Peter's, Rome, windows in attic, engraving

flank the windows and used them in an unexecuted design for the central window on the façade of the Oratory; but he modified them so as to give them a quite new character. In Michelangelo's version the consoles are clearly divided into two parts, to each of which correspond two guttae. Borromini emphasizes this division in the upper part by inserting a diamond-shaped opening in the top, but he divides the lower part into three sections, so that it almost looks like a triglyph. The three grooves of the triglyph, however, lead to the divisions between the four guttae, so that here Borromini returns to Michelangelo's arrangement, but he makes his own variation because he constructs the whole console on a square plan, so that there are four guttae along each side where Michelangelo only has two, and at the bottom of the console he adds a second block of guttae, with two on each face. Finally he decorates the hollows of the 'triglyphs' with a scale motif which Michelangelo uses in the egg-and-tongue decoration of the main entablature of the apse of St Peter's.

The same attic window was the direct source of another motif which Borromini used throughout his life and on which he plays endless variations. In Michelangelo's hands the hood of the window is composed of a shell or an oval opening on either side of which stretches an architrave supported at the ends by the two consoles discussed above. The architrave is completely interrupted by the shell or the opening, which appear to be forcing themselves down through it. When Maderno came to design the façade of the church, he carried on the line of Michelangelo's windows in the attic, but he modified the form by combining the shell and the oval opening

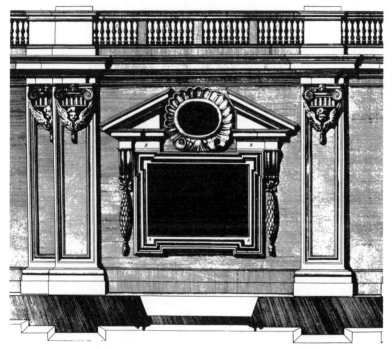

16. Carlo Maderno: St Peter's, Rome, window in attic of façade, engraving

and enclosing them in a pediment, thus softening the effect of thrust, which is characteristic of Michelangelo's design, so that the shell now seems to nestle in the pediment [16]. Further he replaced Michelangelo's massive consoles by conventional curved features from which hang garlands of laurels. At about the same time Flaminio Ponzio produced another variation on the same theme in a blind window on the outer wall of the Palazzo Rospigliosi [17]. He eliminated the consoles and reduced the size of the shell, so that

17. Flaminio Ponzio: Palazzo Rospigliosi, Rome, blind window

18. Borromini: Palazzo Barberini, Rome, window on façade

19 and 20. Borromini: Palazzo Barberini, Rome, details from drawings for façade

it is now comfortably enclosed between the two parts of the architrave. He broke up the rigid rectangle of Michelangelo's frame by
adding projections at the top corners and at the bottom a ledge supported by two dependent rectangular panels decorated with rams'
heads. The effect has decorative charm but the virile quality of the
original has vanished.

Borromini approaches the matter much more boldly, and in the
window on the upper floor of the west façade of the Palazzo Barberini [18], which has already been mentioned, he creates out of
the elements taken from his predecessors a new and completely
Baroque design. In a drawing for the palace, on which characteristically he inserts two different variants of the window on the
two wings [19, 20], he is still close to Maderno and Ponzio, though
he differs from both in using a broken pediment, through which
the shell protrudes, but in the window as actually executed he breaks
away completely from all previous models. He accepts the fact that
the shell creates a curved interruption in the architrave, but he combines the two elements into a single whole by making his architrave
curve up in a semi-circle in the middle to enclose the shell. As a
result he transforms the interrupted movement of his predecessors
into a single continuous swing. He intensifies this movement by
another even more revolutionary gesture: he cants the sides of the
window so that they project at angles of 45° from the surface of
the wall. The architrave is canted with them, so that it takes on
a movement in three dimensions. Borromini enriches this move-

ment by transforming the rectangular projections at the top of Ponzio's window into curved 'ears' through which is threaded a band of laurel, almost neo-classical in its severity. In the middle this passes behind a triglyph with guttae, a motif also taken from Michelangelo. This type of hood was to remain a favourite theme with Borromini and he played variations on it all his life, ending with the most sophisticated versions in the doors of the Collegio di Propaganda Fide [140] and the cloister of S. Carlo alle Quattro Fontane [62].

Another favourite motif of Borromini can also be traced back to Michelangelo, but this time to the Porta Pia [6]. One of Michelangelo's boldest innovations here was to put inside the main straight pediment a curved broken pediment of which the two sections end in volutes. A variant of this motif was used in the central window of the Palazzo dei Conservatori [21], built after his death, in which the inner curved pediment is complete. Borromini uses this design in its inverse, that is to say a curved pediment outside a straight one, in several designs for the monastic buildings of S. Carlo [23], and later in the window on the entrance wall of St John Lateran [98], but he was also inspired by the more ingenious variant produced by Giacomo del Duca in the door of S. Maria in Trivio [22], in which he inverts the Porta Pia design, so that the scrolls come outside the straight pediment and cut into it. Borromini took up Giacomo del Duca's idea, but, as in the Palazzo Barberini window, he fused the elements of his predecessor's schemes into a continuous design and so invented a form of pediment in which the two sections do not interpenetrate but flow easily one into the other. He first used this motif on the facade of the Oratory [24], but it occurs frequently in his later work. Wittkower has pointed out that the pediment has a resemblance to a medieval type of gable which occurred on the façade of the old cathedral of Milan, which was still standing in Borromini's youth, but this differs from Borromini's version in that it consists of a continuous ogee curve, whereas an essential feature of his design is the mixture of straight lines and curves. The designs of Michelangelo and Giacomo del Duca seem to provide a more probable source.

The second authority to which Borromini appealed is the architecture of the Ancients. On one occasion he says explicitly that he had 'imitated the ancients rather than the moderns', and in discussing his projects in the *Opus architectonicum* he constantly refers to ancient buildings which he has used as models, often for some of his more revolutionary innovations.

21. Follower of Michelangelo.
Palazzo dei Conservatori, window,
engraving

22. Giacomo del Duca:
S. Maria in Trivio, Rome, door,
1573–5

23. Borromini: Drawing for garden façade of monastery
of S. Carlo alle Quattro Fontane

24. Borromini: Oratorio di S. Filippo Neri, Rome, façade, after 1638

We know from Martinelli that Borromini studied the remains of ancient Rome with enthusiasm, and he describes a visit which he made with the architect to the Villa Mattei on the Palatine, where they found ruins which Martinelli believed to be the remains of the Portico of Tarquin. He also records that Borromini owned a copy of Pirro Ligorio's *Antichita di Roma*, one of the standard works on the topography of ancient Rome. He almost certainly also knew Ligorio's reconstructions of Hadrian's villa, which, though they bear little resemblance to what the villa is now thought to have looked like, contain many rooms of unusual shapes which would have whetted his appetite. He copied out descriptions of the Golden House of Nero from ancient writers like Suetonius and archaeologists such as Andrea Fulvio, Giacomo Lauri and Vincenzo Scamozzi, and he made a drawing of the garden of Licinius. In his youth he copied details of ancient columns and capitals from an early sixteenth-century sketchbook called the Codex Coner [27], now in the Soane Museum but then in the possession of the Roman collector and antiquarian Cassiano dal Pozzo, who also owned the drawings showing reconstructions of ancient monuments by Giovanni Battista Montano, which Borromini knew and used. Finally there is a drawing by Borromini with a project for restoring the pyramid of Caius Sestius and adapting it as a monument in honour of St Peter and St Paul.

It may at first sight seem strange that an architect who was famous for having broken all the rules accepted since the time of Bramante as being derived from ancient architecture should himself appeal to these very models to justify his innovations; but if we examine the type of ancient architecture on which he drew the problem becomes clearer.

The architects of the sixteenth century had based their principles on the study of Vitruvius and of certain carefully selected examples of Roman architecture. Vitruvius was notoriously conservative, to the extent that he only accepted the Greek orders and excluded the Tuscan and Composite added by the Romans, and Bramante and his followers based their style mainly on the study of either the more classical buildings of ancient Rome, such as the Pantheon, the Temple of Fortuna Virilis and the so-called Temples of Vesta, or on the great structural achievements, such as the Baths or the Basilica of Maxentius, which they called the Temple of Peace. Borromini was instinctively attracted by quite different types of ancient architecture: first the elaborate and exquisitely carved bases and capitals of the Augustan or Flavian periods, which he copied from the Codex Coner, and secondly late Imperial buildings, of which he knew examples at Hadrian's villa at Tivoli and the later Baths, such as those of Diocletian, and apparently others which have now disappeared. There is further a drawing by him at Windsor of a fountain from an ancient nymphaeum [25], formerly in the Giustiniani collection in Rome but now lost, of extreme complexity,

25. Borromini: Drawing after an ancient Roman fountain

which he used as the model for one of his most ingenious designs for a fountain to be made for the Oratory of S. Filippo Neri [40].

We can arrive at more precise conclusions about the ancient architecture which Borromini studied by examining the models which he seems to have imitated in his own works. It is, for instance, clear that he knew the tomb near Capua called the Conocchia [26], one

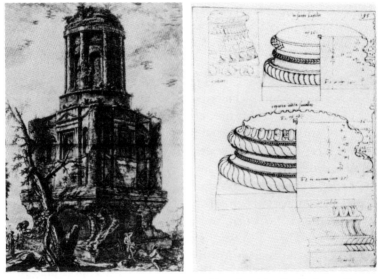

26. Piranesi:
Ancient Roman tomb near Capua,
called the Conocchia

27. Temple of Apollo Sosianus, Rome,
base of column, drawing from Codex Coner
of the early sixteenth century

of the most complex examples of Roman masonry, on which he
based the plan of his dome at S. Andrea delle Fratte [141]; many
details in his treatment of the orders, sometimes the most unconventional features, can also be traced to ancient models. An instance
is his practice of making the flutings on his pilasters irregular, that
is to say, alternately broad and narrow [see, for example, illustration
85], which at first sight seems contrary to all classical practice, but
is in fact to be found in the Augustan Temple of Apollo Sosianus
[27], of which a fragment lay below the Theatre of Marcellus in
the sixteenth and seventeenth centuries and was drawn by the
author of the Codex Coner.

The most spectacular examples of the late Imperial architecture
which Borromini admired are to be found in the Eastern Empire,
for instance at Baalbek, Petra, Sabratha and Leptis Magna, and some
of them are so strikingly like buildings by Borromini that a direct
connection seems inevitable – one of the rock-tombs of Petra [28]

28. El Deir, Petra

29. Temple of Venus, Baalbek

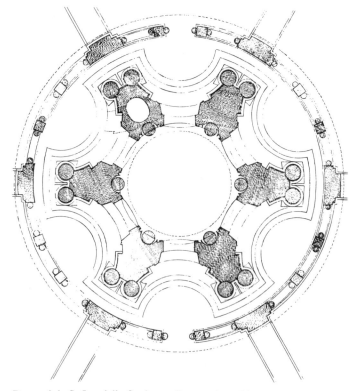

30. Borromini: S. Ivo della Sapienza, Rome, plan of lantern, engraving

has a façade which suggests that of S. Carlo alle Quattro Fontane
[57], and the circular temple at Baalbek [29] is almost identical in plan with the lantern of S. Ivo [30] – but Borromini certainly did not know the buildings of Petra and Sabratha, and it is very doubtful if he saw drawings of those at Baalbek. Sabratha and Leptis Magna were buried under sand till the twentieth century; Petra was not discovered till the mid-nineteenth century; and though Baalbek had been visited by travellers throughout the Middle Ages and in the sixteenth century, there is no evidence to show that adequate drawings were available in Rome in Borromini's day.

It is likely that more buildings of this kind existed in or near Rome in the seventeenth century than are known today, and some of the tombs on the Appian Way, which are now shapeless masses of brickwork, no doubt had more form then, but it seems that Borromini relied for some of his models on an intermediary source of great importance, the drawings of Montano referred to above. Montano's reconstructions appeared in engraved form between 1624 and 1664 in a series of volumes called *Li cinque libri di architettura*, but Borromini probably relied more on the original drawings in Pozzo's collection. The drawings reproduce a number of monuments or details which correspond very closely to general projects or individual features by Borromini. For instance, the exceptionally elaborate fluting used by Borromini in the fireplace of the Sala di Ricreazione at the Oratory of S. Filippo Neri [31], which at first sight one would think a complete invention of his own, can be paralleled exactly in a drawing by Montano of a series of Roman columns [32] – not, incidentally, engraved. Montano also provides the solution to the problem of the similarity between the lantern of S. Ivo and the temple at Baalbek, because one of his drawings [33] shows a building which corresponds in all essentials to the eastern model which Borromini could not have known. The fact that the reconstruction given by Montano is largely based on imagination does not lessen its importance as a source, because it is clear that his versions were taken at their face value by seventeenth-century architects and were regarded as reliable reconstructions of ancient Roman buildings.

Montano's drawings and engravings provide the sources for a number of important motifs in Borromini's buildings which at first sight would not suggest any connection with ancient architecture. Many of the engravings show buildings with façades either on a single concave curve, like S. Agnese in Piazza Navona, or with a combination of concave and convex curves, as at S. Carlo alle Quattro Fontane, though in both cases Borromini has varied the form

31. Borromini: Oratorio di S. Filippo Neri,
detail of fireplace in Sala di Ricreazione

32. G. B. Montano: Roman columns, drawing (detail)

Questo Tempio fu trouato à Tiuoli ricchissimo di ornamenti de quali ue se ne mostra la Cornice e l'ornamento del fregio della parte di fuori contrasegnati cō lettere A et B. et e' di ordine Corinthio.

33. G. B. Montano: Reconstruction of an ancient Roman building, engraving

of the curves and the disposition of the columns shown in Montano's design. More surprising is the fact that Montano shows a building [34] which includes a colonnade with the lines of columns converging and the columns themselves diminishing in size, as in Borro-

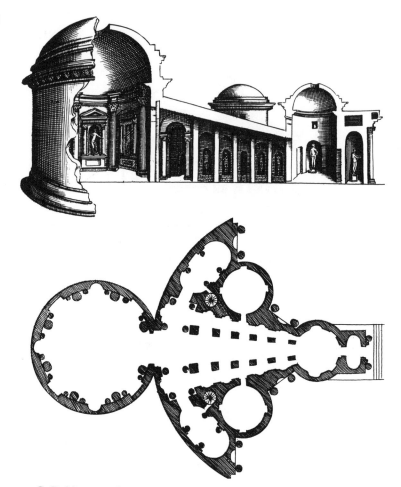

34. G. B. Montano: Reconstruction of an ancient Roman building, engraving

mini's colonnade in the Palazzo Spada [35, 36]. Here, however, the
relation of the imitation to the model is curious, because Borromini's
colonnade is designed so that, seen from the point where the visitor
first becomes aware of it, the effect of perspective greatly increases
its apparent depth, whereas in Montano's design the visitor arrives
at the narrow end of the colonnade and so would be looking, so
to speak, down the wrong end of the telescope. Clearly Montano
did not have the idea of false perspective in mind but merely
recorded something which he had found, or believed he had found,
and it was left to Borromini to adapt his engravings to this novel
purpose.

35 and 36. Borromini:
Palazzo Spada, Rome,
colonnade, and plan

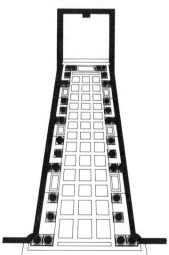

Borromini did not always use such bizarre models, and in one work, the lower part of the campanile of S. Andrea delle Fratte [141], he comes very close to much more classical models. Indeed this work recalls more than any other building the choragic monument of Lysicrates set up in Athens in the middle of the fourth century B.C., but it is unlikely – though not quite impossible – that Borromini should have known drawings of this building. It is more probable that he based his designs on Roman circular structures – such as the Tour de l'Horloge at Aix-en-Provence – one of which is recorded in an ancient relief, now in the Uffizi but in his

37. Roman relief

day built into the wall of the hospital of St John Lateran, of which a copy exists in the volume of drawings by Giuliano da Sangallo, now in the Vatican but in Borromini's day in the Barberini library, to which he certainly had access [37].

There is, however, a third authority to which Borromini appeals in addition to Michelangelo and the Ancients, namely Nature. The idea that architecture is based on nature was a commonplace in the fifteenth and sixteenth centuries, but it took on various different meanings. Some writers turn back to the idea mentioned by Vitruvius that columns imitated the forms of the trees which in primitive times supported the roofs of buildings, and certain architects, such as Bramante in his loggia at S. Ambrogio in Milan, and Philibert de l'Orme in his treatise on architecture, designed columns like trees with the stumps of branches attached to them. More widely held was the doctrine formulated by Vitruvius, and repeated by most

Renaissance writers from Alberti onwards, that the proportions of architecture, and specifically those of the classical columns, were based on the proportions of the human body; Doric on those of a man, Ionic on those of a woman and Corinthian on those of a girl.

With Alberti the theory that architecture imitates nature was combined with the Aristotelian idea that nature is based on laws, and that she tends towards a perfection which she is frustrated from attaining in her individual works by accident. It is the business of the architect – as much as of the painter and sculptor – to seek out this perfection, this harmony, and embody it in his works. Often the harmony underlying nature is associated with the idea of mathematics, either with the Platonic idea that nature is composed of the five regular solids, or with the Pythagorean belief in the eternal value of numerical relations. For Palladio the true proportions of a building were based on certain simple arithmetical relations derived from musical harmony. For Alberti and others the connection was rather with geometry, and they affirmed, for instance, that architects should design churches on a circular plan, because the circle, as the perfect form symmetrical about all axes, was the symbol of the perfection of God.

By the seventeenth century the identification of nature with mathematics had become a widely held belief and it is clearly expressed in the writings of Galileo, who says that 'the great book of nature ... is written in the language of mathematics, and its characters are triangles, circles, and other geometrical figures without which it is humanly impossible to understand a single word of it'. Galileo's writings were much studied in intellectual circles in Rome during Borromini's youth, and it is, I believe, from him that Borromini derived his conception of nature.

If this is so, it would explain a fundamental feature in Borromini's method of work: the fact that he evolved even his most complex and apparently whimsical designs by a series of geometrical manipulations. It has often been pointed out that the plans of S. Carlo alle Quattro Fontane [38, 39] and S. Ivo [81, 83] are based on a series of triangles and circles, but it has not always been sufficiently emphasized that they were actually created out of these geometrical figures. It is not merely that we can impose a neat series of such figures on the plan; we can see from the drawings that the plans were worked out in this way. This is perhaps most clearly visible in the drawings for S. Carlo, where from an early stage the basic geometrical structure is set out. This consists of two equilateral

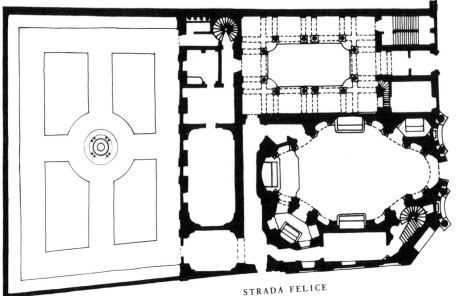

STRADA FELICE

38. Borromini: S. Carlo alle Quattro Fontane, Rome, plan, 1634–41

39. Borromini: S. Carlo alle Quattro Fontane, Rome, diagram of plan

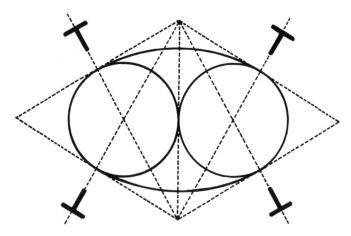

triangles of identical size, placed so that they have one side in common. Circles are inscribed in them, and areas of other circles are drawn with their centres at the ends of the common side. These four form an oval which exactly defines the shape of the dome. So far Borromini is simply following an accepted technique for drawing an oval as it is to be found in Serlio's treatise on architecture and in ordinary seventeenth-century handbooks on geometry; but he goes further and extends the geometrical system to cover the whole plan of the church. The apexes of the triangles fall at the central points of the four bays which surround the central domed space, and lines drawn from the ends of the common side through the centres of the circles define the axes of the subsidiary chapels. In this way the whole of the seemingly complex plan of the church is tied to the basic geometrical scheme.

There are many other examples of Borromini's using this method, one of which is particularly revealing, because it shows that even when he was simply doodling, he doodled in geometrical terms [40]. The drawing consists of a sheet of sketches for a fountain which was planned for the cloister of the Oratory but never carried out. The general form of the fountain is taken from the ancient model formerly in the Giustiniani collection referred to above [25], but

40. Borromini: Drawings for a fountain
for the Oratorio di S. Filippo Neri, Rome

what is interesting is the way Borromini plays variations on the original theme. The fountain is basically formed from a circle, and in some of the variants it is shown surrounded by a circular wall which enclosed the whole area of water. The simplest and probably the first version is that in the top left-hand corner of the sheet. There the fountain consists of a single unit which is repeated four times round the circle. The unit is composed of a straight element, followed by a concave curved bay, which is interrupted in the middle by an almost semi-circular convex bay. This pattern is repeated almost exactly in the version in the bottom left-hand corner, except that a small rectangular break has been inserted at the point where the straight element joins the concavity. This pattern is repeated in the upper middle study, but below are two more complicated variants. In the one at the bottom of the sheet the straight element is interrupted by a further concave bay. In this design the water-spouts, which are indicated by little dots, come alternately outside and inside the enclosing wall of the fountain. In what is presumably the last design, above to the right of the one just discussed, a further wall is introduced which encloses the extra spouts, and at the same time creates a pretty play of contrasting forms, because where the inner wall goes concave the outer is convex and vice versa. The rest of the sheet is filled with elevations of the fountain, which was to stand in the middle of the water, and two plans for a quite different version of the whole scheme.

In the sketches at the top – on the left and in the middle – Borromini has written the figures 1 and 2 against the straight and the concave bays, indicating that he intended these sections to occupy one third and two thirds respectively of the quarter-circle which they fill. This would mean that they would occupy arcs of 30° and 60° respectively. But against the same bays in the lower right-hand sketch he has written 3 and 4, and this would land him in very awkward angles involving sevenths of a right-angle; and it is characteristic of his love of complexity that this was the one he chose and wrote against it: *Si farà questo*.

There is fortunately one piece of direct evidence to confirm the hypothesis that Borromini conceived of architecture in terms of mathematics. It is to be drawn from the letter which he wrote to Cardinal Camillo Pamphili to accompany the designs for his villa. He explains that the villa was to have thirty-two windows placed so that the lines drawn to them from the centre of the building would correspond to the thirty-two points of the compass representing the thirty-two winds, and that four other points in the building would be linked by lines which would represent the tropics of Cancer and Capricorn. There were to be two rooms with hemispherical domes on which the celestial globe could be depicted, as it had been in the Golden House of Nero. Other features would show many things 'which mathematicians teach us from the sphere', and Borromini ends the passage: 'In fact the whole building would be a study in applied mathematics.'

For Borromini the essential link between architecture and nature was, I believe, through mathematics, but on one occasion he refers to a different theory, the familiar idea that architecture was based on the human body. This occurs when he is discussing his design for the curved façade of the Oratory, which, he says, is like a man stretching out his arms to welcome the faithful, and he pursues the parallel further to say that the central bay, which is convex on the lower storey, represents the chest, and the wings are the arms, each wing being composed of two sections at different angles, like the human arm.

This image has nothing to do with Alberti's idea of the relation of architecture to the human figure, which is based purely on the proportions of the body when upright and static. It is, however, closely related to Michelangelo's conception, as it is set out in a famous letter, probably addressed to Cardinal Rodolfo Pio, which shows that he thought of a building as related to a body in movement and in action rather than static. It was this idea that led Michelangelo to break with the tradition of linear and planar architecture current in his day and to create a new conception of the art as something fully three-dimensional and, as it were, living. This quality was certainly among those which Borromini most deeply prized in Michelangelo's buildings, which he studied with such devotion.

From what has been said above it will be clear that there is ample evidence to support Martinelli's estimate of Borromini as an architect who, though full of invention, was well acquainted with the works of the Ancients and the theory of his art. If he deviated from tradition, it was with full knowledge of what he was doing and with a specific purpose in mind. An examination of his works will show how he combined reason with imagination when faced with the problems of actual building.

# S. Carlo alle Quattro Fontane

In 1634 Borromini received his first independent commission, to build the monastery and church of S. Carlo alle Quattro Fontane – generally known, from its small size, as S. Carlino – for the Spanish Order of the Discalced Trinitarians, an austere and poor body of monks whose principal duty was collecting funds to free Christians who had been captured by the Moors.

In the years 1611–12 the Trinitarians had acquired a small site on the south-west corner of the crossing of Strada Pia and Strada

41. Lieven Cruyl: View of Quattro Fontane, Rome,
with S. Carlo on extreme left, drawing, 1665

Felice [41], laid out by Pius IV and Sixtus V, the former, now called Via Venti Settembre, leading from the Quirinal to the Porta Pia, and the latter, now Via delle Quattro Fontane, from the Trinità dei

Monti to S. Maria Maggiore. At the crossing Sixtus had laid out the four fountains which gave the place its name, Quattro Fontane. The monks at first received some financial support from Cardinal Francesco Barberini, whose palace lay diagonally across the Quattro Fontane, but he lost interest and the completion of their plans for building took more than forty years.

In 1634 Borromini designed the wing to contain the lodgings for the monks. It ran from east to west across the middle of the site, so that it was protected from the noise of Strada Pia and only one end of it, which contained vestibules, abutted on Strada Felice. On the ground floor was the refectory, on the first the dormitory, and on the second the library. In February 1635 work was begun on the cloister which occupied the west or right half of the area facing on Strada Pia. Three years later, in 1638, the church was begun, and the structure was finished in the following year. The decoration of the interior was completed in the succeeding years; then the money ran out, nothing further was done, and the façade of the building on Strada Pia remained bare, as can be seen in early drawings. In the years 1662–4 the section of the façade leading to the cloister was stuccoed and the door set up [62], and in 1665 work was begun on the façade of the church [57]. At the time of Borromini's death in 1667 the lower storey was complete and the upper storey probably just begun, but the whole was without sculpture. Work on the façade continued under the direction of Borromini's nephew Barnardo till 1682. Soon after the architect's death the original triangular campanile [41] was pulled down and replaced by the existing tower. Borromini's plans show that he intended to erect a wing along the side of the garden next to Strada Felice, which in one version [45] was to contain a cloister with a series of shallow niches with altars, but this very unusual scheme was not carried out. In the eighteenth century three ranges of undistinguished buildings were erected round the garden.

Borromini was faced with serious limitations owing to the size and shape of the site. The total frontage on Strada Pia, which had to include both the church and the cloister, was less than eighty feet; the site was not rectangular as the two bounding streets ran at a slightly obtuse angle; and the corner of the site at the crossroads was cut off by one of the four fountains. This asymmetry presented great difficulties in the planning of the church, which Borromini overcame brilliantly.

The lay-out of the dormitory block is simple, with the rooms in a single row linked by a passage. The façade on the garden, which was seriously damaged by the eighteenth-century additions to this area, can be reconstructed from Borromini's drawings. The wall surface was austere and only articulated with flat pilaster bands, but the architect planned an ingenious effect on the skyline, where the chimneys were to have the form of the Ionic volutes on pedestals which Michelangelo had used on Porta Pia. Some of the drawings also show a project for a Belvedere in the middle of the roof, where the monks could enjoy the cool of the evening, a regular arrangement in Roman palaces of the time. It was to have been decorated with the type of double pediment discussed in Chapter 2 (p. 34). Internally the only room of interest is the refectory [42], which has rounded corners, a device of which Borromini was to make frequent use in his later works. Its vault is pierced by cross-vaults over

42. Borromini: S. Carlo alle Quattro Fontane, Rome, old refectory, now sacristy, 1634–7

windows and lunettes. The edges of these penetrations are now emphasized by mouldings in stucco, and the field of the vault is decorated by a curved ornament ending in scrolls and panels of foliage which impinge clumsily on the edge of the pointed vaults over the windows, but these are probably additions made – perhaps by Bernardo – when the room was converted into the sacristy in the early years of the eighteenth century, and the vault was almost certainly originally planned like that of the old sacristy. A drawing in the Albertina (221) probably shows Borromini's original design for the ceiling, without the scrolls and foliage but with a decorative panel, centring on a cross, which stands quite free from the window-vaults in the middle of the ceiling.

In the cloister [43] Borromini made brilliant use of the small space available to him. The cloister is basically rectangular, but the architect has introduced variety and movement by cutting off the corners. This he does in a characteristically subtle manner, the corner bays of the lower storey and the balustrade being on a slight curve, convex inwards, and the architrave of the upper storey being straight. The heavy Tuscan Order is appropriate to the rough travertine of which the cloister is constructed, but it is unconventional in detail. Borromini has used the Serlian arch, sometimes called the Palladian arch, with alternating flat and round-headed openings. This is a form much used for cloisters in Lombardy, and Borromini would have known it in Tibaldi's Collegio Borromeo in Pavia [2], which would have been an appropriate model, as the Roman monastery was dedicated to S. Carlo Borromeo. But Borromini made the flat-headed openings wider than usual, simplified the capitals, and reduced the entablature to an abacus-architrave shared by the pairs of columns. Two preliminary drawings (Albertina 195, 196) show that Borromini originally intended to give every arch a keystone in the form of a shield with a cross on it and a crown over it – referring to the symbols of the Trinitarian Order – but in the event he simplified the design and reduced the decoration to two shields with a cross, but without a crown, over the arches at each end of the cloister.

The upper order [43] is again a kind of Tuscan but with octagonal capitals which are more reminiscent of late Gothic architecture than of anything classical. The choice of an octagonal form for the capital enabled Borromini to solve the problem presented by the cut-off corners of the cloister. On the long sides of the cloister the capitals are arranged so that one face is parallel with the plane of the colonnade, but at the point where these sides join the corner sections

the octagonal form allows the architect to have a corner of the capital
on the line bisecting the angle formed by the two parts of the cloister,
defining and articulating the meeting of the two sections.

The most ingenious feature of the whole cloister is the balustrade
on the upper floor [44], where Borromini breaks with every Renaissance convention and introduces the maximum effect of movement

44. Borromini: S. Carlo alle Quattro Fontane, Rome, cloister, detail

and variety into a small detail. Architects of the sixteenth century
always made their balusters circular in plan. Bramante made them
symmetrical about their middle point, but Michelangelo made the
bulge come below the middle, so that the balusters appeared more
stable. Borromini has accepted Michelangelo's break with complete
symmetry, but he has added two innovations: first, the balusters
are not circular in plan but are based on triangles formed of three
slightly concave arcs of circles; secondly, he places the balusters
alternately so that in one the bulge comes at the top and on the
next at the bottom, thus producing an effect of movement rather
than of stability. He used this form of balustrade frequently and,
in discussing his reasons for doing so in the galleries of the Oratory
of S. Filippo Neri, he explains that it allows anyone sitting behind
the balustrade to have the best possible view of what is taking place
below through the gaps between the balusters, a much better view
than if they were circular. He compares the design with the plans
made by military engineers to allow the best fire from behind fortifications, and it is indeed true that in plan his balustrade looks very
like some of Michelangelo's plans for the fortifications of Florence.
These Borromini is unlikely to have known, but it is more than
probable that he studied other works on fortifications in which most
architects of the sixteenth and seventeenth centuries had an interest.
The argument about a clear field of vision does not apply so effectively to the cloister of S. Carlo as to the gallery in the Oratory,
and still less to the altar-rails of the Filomarino altar in Naples or

43. Borromini: S. Carlo alle Quattro Fontane, Rome, cloister, 1634–7

the chapel of S. Giovanni in Laterano, where Borromini uses the same form, and it is legitimate to wonder whether he did not invent the form as much for its ingenuity and effect of movement as for the reason that he gives.

In the middle of the cloister stands a well-head which has the form of an oval enclosed in an octagon and so echoes the shapes of the church and the cloister. Over it is a wrought-iron construction for lowering the bucket, for which a drawing exists on which Borromini sketched out no fewer than ten different projects for this one little feature. The same inventive power appears in his studies for the iron grilles on the windows of the monastery. Clearly he had not lost interest in the designing of ironwork, with which he had been concerned at St Peter's.

The development of the plan of S. Carlino is extremely complex, but accounts of it have been bedevilled by the fact that Hempel, in his otherwise admirable monograph on Borromini, published as preliminary designs for the church three drawings in the Albertina (165, 166, 167) which, it has now been conclusively shown, have nothing to do with it and are probably by Borromini's nephew Bernardo and not by the artist himself. If these drawings are set aside, it is possible to deduce from the true preparatory drawings in the Albertina the actual evolution of Borromini's plan, but this is not easy, because in some cases the architect has worked over the plans so many times and with such heavy black chalk that it is extremely difficult to decipher the lower layers of the palimpsest.

The key drawing is Albertina 171 [45]. This shows the whole area covered by the monastery drawn in a precise manner, with clear ruled outlines and even shading. It is just possible to discern under the later emendations the form which the church had in this redaction. This consists of a central space in the form of an elongated octagon, to which are added on the longer axis rectangular elements for a vestibule and choir. The arrangement on the shorter axis is not so easy to decipher, but there are fairly clear indications that there were two similar rectangular chapels, each forming a kind of transept. The hypothesis that this was the original form of the church is strengthened by the fact that on another sheet among the Albertina drawings (178) Borromini has drawn out exactly this form next to a drawing of a quarter of the church, including the chapel to the left of the High Altar, in its final form, as if he wished to compare the ultimate complex solution with its simple embryo.

Borromini evidently found his first plan unsatisfactory and he gave it greater richness and variety in the next version by making

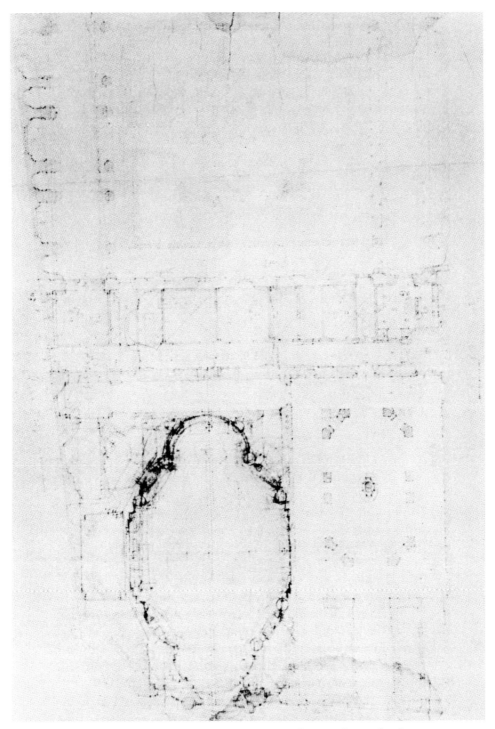

45. Borromini: Plan for S. Carlo alle Quattro Fontane, Rome, drawing

all the members outside the central octagonal space semi-circular instead of rectangular [46]. At this stage, no doubt prompted by the Fathers, Borromini seems to have become aware of the fact that his plans did not include adequate provision for a sacristy – indeed it is hard to see where he could have included one sufficient for the needs of the church – and he solved this problem neatly by moving the whole axis of the church to the west and at the same time replacing the semi-circular 'transepts' by shallow curved elements, which

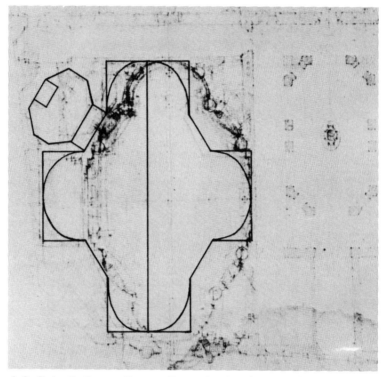

46. S. Carlo alle Quattro Fontane, Rome, drawing shown on illustration 45 with Borromini's second scheme strengthened

allowed him to insert a reasonably sized sacristy between the church and the eastern edge of the site. By this stage the main outlines of the church as it exists today had been fixed, but in the last overdrawings on this sheet and in various other drawings Borromini evolved more and more complex forms [47, 48] for the various elements of the design, particularly for the section lying between the semi-circular apse and vestible and the flattened 'transepts'.

Under the church is a crypt [49] which has almost exactly the same size and shape as the upper church, but is simpler because

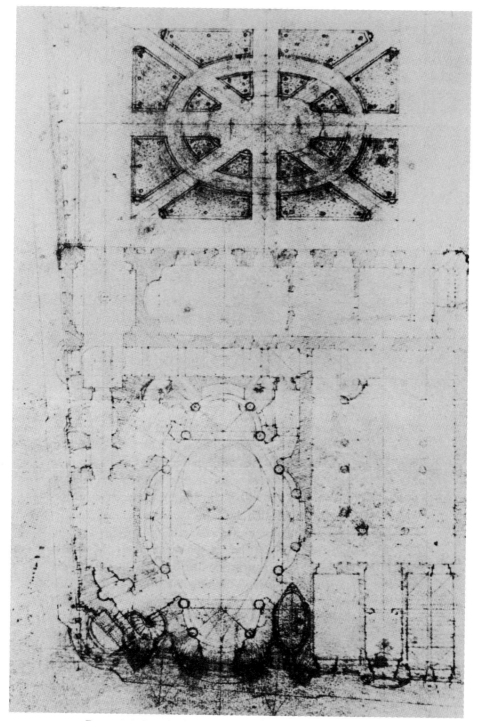

47. Borromini: Plan for S. Carlo alle Quattro Fontane, Rome, drawing

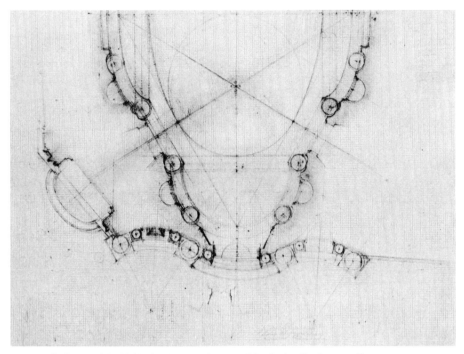

48. Borromini: Half plan for the church of S. Carlo alle Quattro Fontane, Rome, drawing

the walls are only articulated by very flat pilaster bands, which support a low vault pierced by cross-vaults over lunettes, though we know from a drawing (Albertina 180) that at one stage Borromini intended to put columns in the semi-circular chancel and behind the High Altar. In spite of its extreme simplicity the effect is one of absolutely controlled spatial harmony.

The lower church is closed on the west side, but on the east side there are two chapels, a larger one on the main cross-axis, which is of little interest, and a much smaller one in the south-east corner which Borromini may have designed for his own burial place [50]. In plan this chapel is an octagon, which at first sight looks regular, though in fact the four sides on the main axes are slightly larger than those on the diagonals. Each bay encloses a niche, but those on the larger sides, being made proportionate to their width, are taller than the others and break through the entablature as far as the cornice, whereas the smaller ones are covered by a complete entablature. The result is that the cornice, which runs continuously round the whole chapel, makes a curve of incredible complexity.

49. Borromini: S. Carlo alle Quattro Fontane, Rome, Lower Church, 1637–41

50. Borromini: S. Carlo alle Quattro Fontane, Rome, chapel in Lower Church

Seen in elevation it is simply a regular wave or extended S-curve, but, owing to the fact that some of the bays are convex, it takes on a three-dimensional twist, which creates an effect of variety and movement which few other architects could have created in such a small and apparently simple chapel.

The church itself [51] is even more complex. The geometrical manipulations by which Borromini arrived at the plan have been discussed in the last chapter, but the complexities introduced in the execution are manifold. The first impression produced on the spectator will probably be of the flowing movement of the walls – composed of shallow and deep curved bays linked by straight elements – but the movement is not simply on the surface. The wall is treated in an almost sculptural manner, reminiscent of Michelangelo. It is articulated with columns set into the walls so that they form strong supporting elements but do not interrupt the movement of the walls. The middle zone is cut into by niches of varying sizes, the larger ones containing statues. Below these larger niches are doors leading to the side-chapels, the staircase to the bell-tower and the monastic buildings. The altars themselves are designed without columns or pilasters and therefore do not in any way conflict with the dominant effect of the columns. The entablature runs uninterruptedly round the church and over it comes a zone composed of the four coffered half-domes of the choir and main chapels, and between them four broad pendentives decorated with oval panels in low relief, surrounded by winged cherubs which fill the triangular spaces left between the half-domes and the reliefs. Above this comes a heavily moulded oval ring, which supports the balustrade composed of stiffly carved leaves, below each of which is a cross, the symbol of the Trinitarian order. From the oval ring springs the dome [52], at the top of which is a lantern lit by large windows which throw light downwards into the church and upwards on to the symbol of the Holy Trinity on the vault of the lantern itself.

How Borromini calculated the heights of these various parts of the elevation must for the moment remain an open question, because, curiously enough, there are no surviving drawings of elevations or sections in his own hand. Some writers have suggested that the elevations were worked out on a system of triangulation, like that used by medieval masons – a tradition with which Borromini would have been familiar, because the district of Lombardy from which he came was the home of these masons – and one critic has produced diagrams to show that an equilateral triangle drawn with its base on the long axis of the church would reach to the top of

51. Borromini: S. Carlo alle Quattro Fontane, Rome, interior, 1637–41

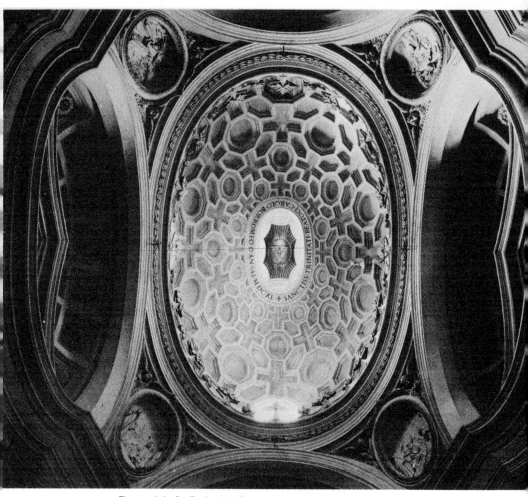

52. Borromini: S. Carlo alle Quattro Fontane, Rome, dome

the entablature, but there are no accurate measured drawings of the church on which to check this, and in the case of S. Ivo della Sapienza, of which measured engravings made in the early eighteenth century are available, the system of triangulation does not seem to work.

An interesting feature of the disposition of the walls of the church is that they can be read in two different ways. If we concentrate on the zone from the entablature upwards, the church is seen as being composed of four concave bays linked by straight elements; but if we forget the entablature and examine the walls below it, the dominant feature is a sort of triptych, composed of a central bay, with a door and a tall niche, flanked by two bays only broken by a small niche. In this way a subtle counterpoint is set up, but it is so slight as not to disturb the harmony of the whole church. It is sometimes said that there is a certain conflict or even contradiction between the complexity of the lower parts of the walls and the simple oval of the dome; but this can be seen differently as a deliberate progression from the complexity of the wall zone, through the relative simplicity of the pendentive zone, to the pure oval of the dome.

In using a basically oval plan Borromini was following a tradition which had been growing in importance since the mid-sixteenth century. Peruzzi and Serlio had invented several ingenious designs based on a simple oval, but they were not carried out. Vignola had used an oval dome over a rectangular substructure at S. Andrea sulla via Flaminia (1550–53), and in his later S. Anna dei Palafrenieri (begun 1565) he made the body of the church itself oval. In S. Giacomo degli Incurabili (begun just before 1590) Francesco da Volterra followed his example, but on a much larger scale.

The earliest of these churches was built while the Council of Trent was still sitting, and the others were put up during the decades when its influence was being most directly felt in Rome, and it is likely that the use of the oval plan may have been dictated partly by liturgical requirements. The Council and its interpreters laid great stress on the worship of the Holy Sacrament, which was now kept in a special tabernacle on the altar instead of in a cupboard (or aumbry) as in earlier times, and the faithful were encouraged to sit and contemplate it. For this purpose a compact plan was more suitable than a Latin Cross, and it is no accident that centralized or near-centralized plans – oval or rectangular – were so frequently used in the seventeenth century. Borromini used this form regularly throughout his career, at S. Carlino, the Oratory, S. Maria dei Sette Dolori, the chapel of Propaganda Fide, and at S. Ivo, but he made his own highly ingenious variations on it. Even in the simple rectangular chapels – the Oratory, S. Maria dei Sette Dolori and Propaganda Fide – he replaces the sharp corners by curves, so that the walls seem to form a continuous surface which, as it were, envelops the worshippers in the church. At S. Carlino this effect is achieved with even greater effect by the establishment of a series of curved and straight surfaces which constitute a wall of movement. At S. Ivo Borromini develops the movement to an even further point and applies it to a completely centralized building. The ingenuity and effectiveness of these variations can be seen by a comparison with the simple, almost elementary, oval of Francesco da Volterra's S. Giacomo degli Incurabili [53].

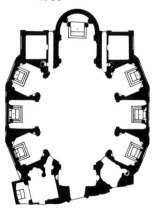

53. Francesco da Volterra: S. Giacomo degli Incurabili, Rome, plan, *c.* 1590

At S. Carlino Borromini showed great skill in the planning of the small chapels. Of the four spaces on the diagonal axes of the church one was occupied by the staircase leading up to the belfry and down to the lower church, and another, diagonally opposite it, by the way through to the monastic buildings. At the two ends of the second diagonal Borromini intended to have chapels. For the one on the left of the High Altar, which was to have been given to Cardinal Francesco Barberini, he experimented with a great variety of forms, shown on a drawing (Albertina 174), finally settling on a simple hexagonal plan without any curves. This he was able to place so that the altar of the chapel was on its main axis and so faced into the central space of the church, but in the opposite corner the area available for a chapel was restricted and awkward in shape and Borromini was compelled to place his chapel, which is also hexagonal, so that it is entered through one of the smaller sides and the altar is on the left, against the wall backing on to the cloister.

The decoration of the church is also extremely original. As is his almost invariable rule, Borromini uses no colour beyond the painted altarpieces with their gilt frames and stucco panels above and below the large niches; all the rest is of white stucco, broken only by the dark of the wrought-iron grilles to the chapels [54], which are only just touched with gilding. Everything is achieved by the design of the detail. The order is composite, but in half the capitals the volute

54. Borromini: S. Carlo alle Quattro Fontane, Rome, grille of side-chapel

55 a and b. Borromini: S. Carlo alle Quattro Fontane, Rome, interior, capitals

is inverted [55a and b], giving the impression at first sight that it is a kind of Corinthian, an unorthodox variation which Borromini took from models at Hadrian's Villa. The niches all have shell-heads, but of a highly personal type: in the larger niches flame-like tongues protrude from behind the shells [56a], and the smaller ones are divided into three sections, almost like the sections of an orange [56b]. Everywhere Borromini uses the winged cherubs in which he was to rejoice all his life. They support the bigger niches, at the same time carrying roundels; they carry garlands of leaves over the altarpiece; and they fill the triangular gaps round the reliefs in the pendentives. The decoration of the dome [52] is a form of coffering based on a pattern which goes back ultimately to an early Christian mosaic on the vault of S. Costanza, of which a variant was engraved by Serlio, but Borromini was the first architect to use it in three dimensions and on a dome rather than on a barrel-vault.

There is also a hint in the decoration of the symbolism which Borromini was to develop more explicitly in his later works. The cross, which is one of the symbols of the Trinitarian Order, appears in the coffering of the dome, in the iron gates closing the chapel and also in some of the drawings for the decoration, where it is com-

56 a and b. Borromini: S. Carlo alle Quattro Fontane, Rome, niches

bined with the symbol of the Trinity. A further drawing for the frame of one of the altarpieces shows it composed of palm trees bent over into the form of a broken arch. This, combined with the winged cherubs, is almost certainly an allusion to the decoration of the Holy of Holies in the Temple of Jerusalem, which contained these elements. The Holy of Holies and the entire Temple of Solomon were described and illustrated in the commentary on Ezekiel by the two Jesuits Girolamo Prado and Giovanni Villalpando, whose work appeared between 1596 and 1604 and was keenly studied by seventeenth-century architects. Palms and cherubs' heads, as well as the cross and the crown of eternal life, also appear on the façade.

As has already been said, the façade [57] was not begun till 1665, and it has always been assumed that the design dates from the same period. Indeed, on the basis of the drawings which are now known not to be for S. Carlino, it was believed that initially Borromini intended to have a straight front with four free-standing columns. However, an examination of the drawings which are actually connected with the church shows that this is not the case and that from the beginning he planned a curved façade, an idea which was very advanced for the mid-1630s.

In the drawing [45] on which we can trace the early stages of Borromini's designs for the church the façade is clearly indicated. The central bay contains the door which is flanked by columns, but otherwise the front is entirely composed of flat elements, either pilasters or pilaster bands. The side bays each have a niche in the middle, but the interesting feature about them is that, though the section outside the niche is parallel to the main plane of the façade, the inner one slopes fairly sharply forward towards the door. This involves a breach with the tradition followed by all architects up to and including Maderno, that a church façade should be designed in parallel planes, even when, as at S. Andrea sulla via Flaminia or S. Giacomo degli Incurabili, it leads to an oval interior.

The next drawing to be considered [58] only shows the façade and the part of the church immediately behind it. Like the last it must date from an early stage in the evolution of the church design, because the arrangement of the interior of the church is quite different from that in the actual building. Borromini has taken as his starting point the fact that the corner of the site is cut off by the fountain which he has incorporated in the design by establishing

58. Borromini: S. Carlo alle Quattro Fontane, Rome,
design for façade and towers, drawing

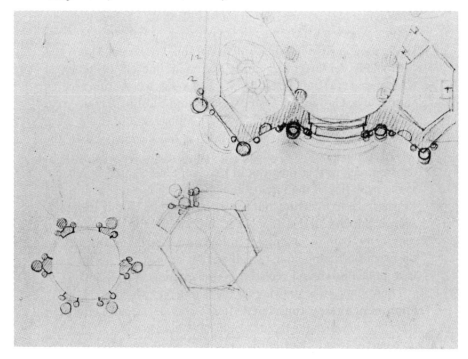

57. Borromini: S. Carlo alle Quattro Fontane, Rome, façade

a balancing section on the right of the building, thus giving the basis for a symmetrical design. Between these two bays he has constructed a central element consisting of a convex middle section for the door, flanked by two bays which project in such a way that they are mirror-images of the outer sections, except that they are on a slight concave curve which, running on through the middle of the convex section, gives the double S-curve which is the most remarkable feature in the façade as it stands today. The façade was to be articulated by six large columns at the points where the line of the front changes direction, with pairs of smaller columns between them, of which those in the inner bays flank niches. This arrangement implies for the middle section of the front an elevation very close indeed to that of the church as actually built, with a smaller Order playing against a larger, as in Michelangelo's Capitoline palaces.

There is, however, one detail in this plan which suggests that, if it had been followed, the façade would have differed fundamentally from the building as we know it today. The left-hand bay of the design was evidently intended to support the bell-tower which comes at this point in the actual building, and it is clear that Borromini was already thinking about it, because the drawings include two studies for it. But the plan is so obviously, one might almost say aggressively, symmetrical that it is difficult to escape the conclusion that at this stage Borromini was planning a façade with two towers, a pattern which, though not common in Italy, had been recently used in Rome in the churches of the Trinità dei Monti and S. Atanasio dei Greci and which Borromini himself was to use at S. Agnese [114] and possibly in the designs for the unexecuted church of S. Giovanni di Dio or S. Giovanni Calabita, known from drawings (Albertina 356, 358, 359). What would have been exceptional, however, is the fact that, as the drawing shows, the towers would have been hexagonal, with an angle, not a flat surface, on the street, so that they would have appeared canted in relation to the main line of the façade, an effect which is not found in any Renaissance architecture, but occurs in some late Gothic churches, such as the cathedral at Ingolstadt, and was used in the eighteenth century by Baroque architects in Portugal, Brazil and Mexico. In the event Borromini built a single triangular tower [41], which was later pulled down and replaced by the existing square belfry.

There is one other drawing for the façade [59] which stands apart from those already considered. It shows four variants of a plan according to which the façade would have consisted of a single concave curve. It is related to the drawing just discussed in that the

59. Borromini: S. Carlo alle Quattro Fontane, Rome, drawing for façade

façade is articulated with large and small columns, but these are arranged in a quite different way, with a single large column flanked by two small ones in each side bay. Further, in this plan the fountain is not incorporated into the façade, but is treated as a separate bay, as in the actual building. One of the most interesting features of this sheet of drawings is that it contains the only surviving sketches for the elevation of the façade. They show that at this stage Borromini would not have divided the lower storey so emphatically into two sections as he did in the actual building. The door was to be enclosed in an arch which would have come up to the main entablature and so would have broken the strong line of the entablature carried by the smaller order of columns. The drawing also shows that the upper storey was to be considerably less high than the lower, and that the order just enclosed the oval window which corresponds to the opening in the aedicula of the actual façade and would presumably have opened internally on the half-dome over the entrance. The façade would have ended in the double pediment which Borromini had planned to use for the belvedere over the dormitory-wing of the monastery. This design would have fitted better with the elevation of the corner over the fountain than does the existing façade, since the upper storey would have been close in scale to the attic on the latter.

It is, of course, unthinkable that an architect of Borromini's integrity and inventiveness should have simply taken his old sketches out of a drawer and used them as they stood when in 1665 the building of the façade became a real possibility, and in fact there is one drawing [47] on which he seems to have redrawn the façade in the form that it actually has today. What is important, however, is that in the mid-1630s he was planning a façade on a curved plan, or rather that he was playing with several alternative plans all involving curves.

This is relevant to the question on which so much time and thought has been wasted: who was the first architect to think of building a church façade on a curved plan? The dates are so difficult to determine that no clear answer is possible. The prize probably goes to Pietro da Cortona, because the façade of SS. Luca e Martina was actually begun in 1635, but Borromini may have been planning a façade for S. Carlino at any time after 1634, when he received the commission for the whole monastery. The point, however, is not material, because clearly several architects were brooding on this problem at the same time and almost certainly exchanged ideas about it. Further, the preliminary steps towards curving the façade of a church had been taken long before. The outer side of Antonio da Sangallo's Porta di S. Spirito is slightly concave, as is the fountain on the corner of the Casino of Julius III on the Via Flaminia, and Ricchino had given a much bolder example of the form in the Collegio Elvetico in Milan [4], begun in 1629, though it is not certain that this was known in Rome. Cortona himself had already used curves, though on a small scale, at the Vigna Sacchetti. Moreover, seen in the context of the general development of the design of church façades in the later sixteenth and early seventeenth centuries, one can say that in S. Susanna Maderno had gone as far as was possible in introducing movement into a façade composed entirely in parallel planes, and it can be seen as a logical step that Baroque architects of the generation of Cortona and Borromini in their pursuit of movement should break away from the plane and design their façades in terms of curves.

What is much more interesting than to determine priority is to examine the different ways in which the various Baroque architects applied the new idea, but it will be more convenient to postpone this problem till we have examined the other façades built by Borromini.

Since it is known that the façade of S. Carlino was not finished till long after Borromini's death, it is necessary to examine whether it was completed according to his designs. There is no direct evidence about this because no drawings exist for the final version and the documents do not throw any light on the matter. There are, however, certain features of the building itself which are disquieting.

We need not be concerned about the lower storey, because it was finished – except for the sculpture – before Borromini's death, but the upper storey needs careful examination.

There is nothing uncharacteristic of Borromini in the general articulation of the storey with tall and short columns, which echo those on the lower stage, but it is possible to question whether he would have repeated exactly the same order on two superimposed storeys. At the Oratory, as we shall see, where he was compelled to use two giant orders, he differentiated them quite clearly. The oval aedicula in the middle bay of the façade of S. Carlo is entirely typical, though it recalls most closely some of Borromini's tombs in the Lateran dating from the pontificate of Alexander VII and is, therefore, almost certainly an addition made when the final designs were produced in 1665. The most uncharacteristic part of the design is the crowning feature of the façade, with its entablature and balustrade interrupted by a panel of fresco supported by flying angels and covered by a scroll in the form of an ogee arch. As far as we know Borromini never incorporated paintings into his architecture in this way, and the ogee scroll has no parallel in his work. It therefore seems likely, on general stylistic grounds, that this feature was an insertion by Bernardo. What almost clinches the matter is that the panel with the angels is taken exactly from Bernini, who had used this arrangement in the High Altar of the church of S. Tommaso da Villanova at Castel Gandolfo. It is unthinkable that Borromini in his last years should have borrowed in this way from his hated rival. It is on the other hand in character with the conduct of affairs at S. Carlino under Bernardo. In 1675 he gave the commis-

60. Borromini: S. Carlo alle Quattro Fontane, Rome, niche on façade

sion for the statue of S. Carlo Borromeo, which was to stand in the central niche of the façade [60], to one of Bernini's most successful pupils, Antonio Raggi, and, though nothing – beyond their names – seems to be known of the sculptors who executed the other statues and the decorative sculpture on the façade, some at least seem to show signs of training in the tradition of Bernini.

ASPECTVS INTERIOR TEMPLI | S.CAROLI AD QVATVOR FONTES
EQ FRANCISCO | BORROMINO ARCHITECTO

61. Borromini: S. Carlo alle Quattro Fontane, Rome, section, engraving

The suspicion that this crowning feature is not of Borromini's devising is confirmed if we examine the relation of the upper storey of the façade to the church itself [61]. Up to the oval aedicule it is connected with the building and the opening in the aedicule corresponds with a window in the half-dome over the entrance; but above this all connection ceases and the façade rises as a free-standing wall, unrelated to what lies behind it. As will appear from later examples, Borromini was not always clear in his method of relating exterior to interior, but there is no instance of such a gross breach of structural logic.

Until further evidence is discovered in the form of drawings or documents we have no means of reconstructing Borromini's original design, but as a pure hypothesis it may be suggested that he intended the second storey to be less high – as in the early drawing for the elevation of the façade – and that it was to have had in the middle an opening linked to the window at the bottom of the dome. In this way the façade would have been rationally related to the interior of the church, the exact repetition of the order would have been avoided, and the dome, which is at present totally obscured by the façade, would have been at least partially visible. Furthermore this arrangement would correspond closely to that used by Michelangelo in the attic of St Peter's, where the openings in the outer walls give light to windows in the vaults of the apses which are separated from them by a gap of some fifteen feet.

As it stands today the façade – or at least the lower half of it – is more mature than any of the schemes evolved for it by Borromini in the 1630s, but it is closely related to them. In plan he has taken the central section of the scheme shown in Illustration 45 but has eliminated the straight elements and fused the whole into a continuous double S-curve, which is perhaps the most complete expression of the Baroque desire for movement to be found in any church façade. The central convex bay of the façade, which follows the bulge visible in the drawing of the façade in its uncompleted form, expresses very clearly the form of the semi-circular bay behind it and, although the same cannot be said of the concave side bays, they are related to the interior by a different kind of link, for, as appears in what seems to be a fair copy of the final scheme, the arcs of these bays are drawn with the same radius as the semi-circular bay of the entrance vestibule. This link is only established at the very last stage, when Borromini decided to replace the straight elements on his earlier design by curves, but it ties the façade and the interior together in a much more intimate manner.

The dome is of a type unusual in Rome but normal in Lombardy, where the cupola is often enclosed in a cylinder of masonry which takes the lateral thrust and avoids the need for buttresses. At S. Carlino it only narrows at the very top in three steps – an echo of the stepping on the dome of the Pantheon – which lead up to the

lantern. This is oval in plan like the dome, with six curved re-entrant
bays of varying widths separated by single Tuscan columns, that is
to say, an oval version of the type of rotunda which, as we have
seen, occurs in the circular temple at Baalbek and in one of Montanus' drawings. The lantern ends in a typically Borrominesque
manner with further steps, on the top of which stands the orb of
the world dominated by the cross. The re-entrant bays are echoed,
though in slightly flattened form, on the interior of the lantern,
where they create a shield-like form on which is the dove of the
Holy Ghost set against the triangle of the Trinity.

Borromini is responsible for one other addition to the complex
of S. Carlo alle Quattro Fontane, the decoration of the front of the
monastic buildings on Strada Pia, which was carried out in 1662-4.
In the main this consisted of a pattern of flat stucco bands which
linked together the rather irregularly disposed windows into a
coherent pattern, but there are two more important features which
emphasized the central axis: at the top of the façade a coat-of-arms
with the cross of the order supported by two stucco angels, and on
the ground floor a door [62] which was the main entrance to the
monastery.

The door is exceptionally ingenious in design. It stands above
three steps which are curved at the ends but flattened in the middle,
no doubt because the street is so narrow that no further projection
would have been allowed. The curves of the steps are taken up in
the jambs of the door, which have deep mouldings typical of Borromini. The most remarkable part of the design is, however, the hood.
In elevation this seems to be merely a variant of the form which
Borromini had used in his early years in the window on the Palazzo
Barberini, but it is in fact more complex. The Barberini window
consisted of a central section flat against the wall, with two jambs
which projected from it at angles of 45°. At S. Carlino the whole
hood is curved in plan, so that it forms a continuous three-
dimensional curve, which fuses the elements of the earlier design
into a single whole, just as the final design for the façade of the
church gave unity and continuity to the interrupted movement of
the earlier designs partly composed of straight lines, partly of
curves. Seen in elevation, the design is also original and effective.
It consists of a central circular panel, which originally contained
a mosaic surrounded by winged cherubs' heads which rest on top
of the door and support the medallion, so forming an architectural
link between the door and the hood itself. This use of sculpture

performing the function of architecture is a characteristic feature of Borromini's mature style, but rarely did he apply it with such brilliant success.

Even here, however, Borromini has not abandoned his habit of working through geometry. A section of the cornice given in an

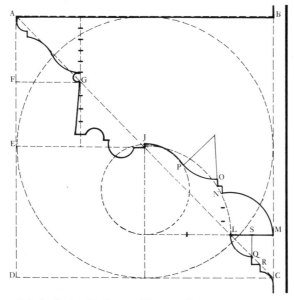

63. Borromini: S. Carlo alle Quattro Fontane, Rome,
section of moulding of door to cloister, section

early eighteenth-century engraving shows the system on which the mouldings were based [63]. The whole cornice is enclosed within a square ABCD. The side AD is divided into halves and quarters at F and E. These give J and G at the points a quarter and half way along the diagonal AC, which mark the main breaks in the moulding. The lower half of the moulding depends on the proportions of 1 : 2 and 1 : 3. For instance, the radius of the arc JP is one sixth of the side of the square, and the same radius is used for the arcs PO and NM. A circle of double this radius, i.e. one third of the side of the square, runs through the points J, O, N, L. The lengths of LS, SM and SQ are all equal, and the arc LQ has a radius of one twelfth of the side of the square. Finally, all the crucial points in the moulding – G, J, L, Q and R – lie on the diagonal AC.

S. Carlino established Borromini's reputation, at least among a small group of enthusiastic admirers, as an architect who combined skill in design with economy in expense. The Trinitarian Father

62. Borromini: S. Carlo alle Quattro Fontane, Rome, door to cloister, 1662–4

who wrote the official account of the church describes the effect which the building produced in Rome. He begins by praising it for exactly those qualities which Martinelli had picked out in his *elogium* of Borromini, saying that 'nothing could be found as ingenious (*artificioso*), fantastic (*capriccioso*), rare or extraordinary', but adds that the whole work was 'well founded on the antique and on the writings of the best architects'. He goes on to speak, perhaps in somewhat exaggerated terms, of the interest which the church aroused and says that the monks received requests for drawings of it from many foreigners, including Germans, Flemings, Frenchmen, Italians, Spaniards and even Indians. Borromini, he rightly says, would have derived great profit from having the plans engraved, but this he refused to do as he was not interested in money – and the author adds that he refused all fees for building S. Carlino – and was too busy with other work. The Spanish ambassador, the Marquis of Castelrodrigo, was so much impressed with the building that he promised twenty-five thousand crowns for the façade, a promise which he was prevented from keeping because he was called back to Spain before the church was finished; and several official bodies, including the Oratorians and the authorities of the University of Rome, were persuaded by the example of S. Carlino to give the commission for their own buildings to Borromini. The Trinitarian Father ends his account of the building by praising Borromini for the care with which he supervised the actual construction: 'He guided the builder's shovel, the plasterer's darby, the carpenter's saw, the stonemason's chisel, the brick-layer's trowel and the iron-worker's file, with the result that the quality of his work is high but not the cost, as his detractors claim, and this all springs from his intelligence and his industry.'

# ✻✻4✻✻

# *The Oratory of S. Filippo Neri and the Filomarino Altar*

In 1637, when Borromini was just about to start work on the church of S. Carlino, he was commissioned to build the Oratory of S. Filippo Neri, also called the Oratory of the Filippini [24], the principal Roman house of the Oratorian order. The commission was of far greater importance than that for S. Carlino, but the difficulties involved in it were so great that the resultant building, though it contains many fascinating and splendid parts, is not as a whole one of the architect's most satisfactory achievements. A study of the building can, however, throw a great deal of light on Borromini's methods because of the detailed account given in the *Opus architectonicum* of his plans and intentions and of the factors which prevented them from being executed according to his wishes.

The Oratory was founded by Filippo Neri in 1561 as an informal gathering of men of piety and good will, on the model of the Oratory of Divine Love formed forty years earlier by S. Gaetano Thiene, one of the first manifestations of the reforming spirit within the Church of Rome. Filippo Neri had already devoted many years to work among the poor and sick of Rome, and charity and love of one's neighbour were his guiding principles, but he also believed in the value of learning and the arts, and he wished his teaching to be spread among all classes of society, rich and poor, learned and ignorant, rulers and servants. For this reason he did not want to found an enclosed order, but he and his companions continued to move in the world, though living lives of the utmost simplicity; and he intended that their teaching and their preaching should be based on sound knowledge and should employ the arts of persuasion, particularly that of music. He was a close friend of the composer Palestrina, one of the greatest exponents of the musical reform which accompanied the religious reform, and many of Palestrina's works were written for the Oratorians.

As originally formed in 1561 the Oratory was a quite informal gathering of men with common ideas, who met in the Convent of S. Girolamo della Carità and later moved to rooms attached to S. Giovanni dei Fiorentini, but in the Holy Year of 1575 it was established as a Congregation with the full approval and support of Gregory XIII, who handed over to it the church of S. Maria in Vallicella, near Monte Giordano, together with the buildings of a small Franciscan convent near by. It was decided to start by rebuilding the church, as the most important part of the complex, and the foundation stone was laid on 15 September 1575. The original plan of the church, now generally known as the Chiesa Nuova, may have been made by Neri's favourite architect, Matteo di Città di Castello, but the conduct of the building was entrusted to Martino Longhi the Elder, one of the most successful practitioners in a somewhat bleak phase of Roman architecture. The façade was added by Fausto Rughesi in 1605, and the decoration of the interior continued till after the middle of the seventeenth century. Meanwhile the members of the congregation continued to use the cramped quarters of the old convent.

Filippo Neri died in 1595, before the church was finished and before any plans for expanding the buildings of the Oratory had been made, but it had always been an essential part of his project to include a library and an oratory where musical performances could be given. In 1611 it was realized that the site occupied by the Fathers, which was to the east of the church, was too small to allow of serious expansion and that land must be acquired to the west. With the help of a papal bull the necessary expropriations were carried out, and in 1621 a new sacristy was begun projecting to the west from the left transept of the church, which is, incidentally, sited so that the High Altar is at the north end. According to the documents this sacristy, the existence of which was to be a great embarrassment when the designs for the whole Oratory came to be prepared, was begun by Mario Arconio in 1621, but mainly built by Paolo Maruscelli between 1629 and 1631.

A few years later plans were invited for the completion of the building, and those of Maruscelli were chosen. His designs, which were much bolder and much more lucidly worked out than any of those by his competitors, were based on the idea of making an almost completely rectangular block by cutting right across the existing islands of buildings in order to make the main front of the building continue the line of the church façade. This involved clearing away the irregular line of houses to the west of the site and cutting a new street to the east of the church through the area formerly occupied by the Fathers. For some reason, however, Maruscelli was not thought competent to carry out this plan alone and in 1637 Borromini was appointed co-architect with him, with the result that after a few months Maruscelli resigned, leaving Borromini in sole charge.

Basically the plan which existed when Borromini took charge [64] consisted of two cloisters, a small one south of the sacristy, round which were grouped the oratory, library and guest rooms which had to be accessible to visitors, and a larger one to the north for the

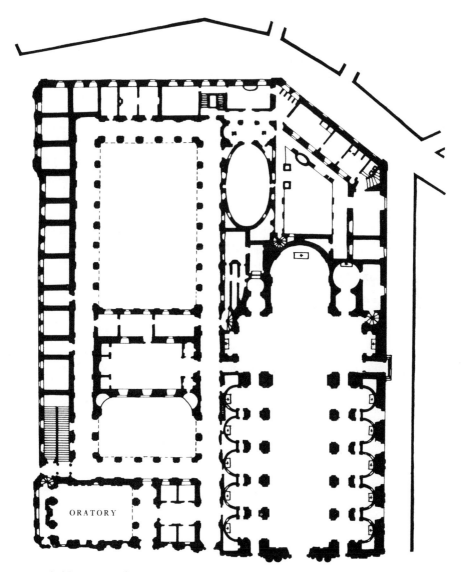

64. Borromini: Oratorio di S. Filippo Neri, Rome, 1637, plan

habitation of the Fathers. These two parts were linked by a long corridor which led from the main entrance next to the church along the loggias of the two cloisters to the north wing of the building, and so formed the spine of the whole complex. In the wing between the south court and the street was the oratory, that is to say, the room devoted to the performance of music, to which the founder of the order attached great importance, and which gave its name to the whole institution and to the word *oratorio* in its musical sense. The first works of this kind, composed for St Philip himself, were by Emilio Cavalieri and Palestrina, but in Borromini's time the chief composer active for the Oratory was Giacomo Carissimi, whose *Historiae sacrae*, which included costumes, action and sometimes dancing, exactly satisfied the requirements of the Fathers.

Originally the oratory was to be placed at the left (west) end of the main front of the building, but this had the disadvantage that the space which it occupied did not correspond to the central part of the façade on the street. To remedy this defect Borromini first tried moving the oratory to the middle of the street front, where it could be logically worked into a symmetrical design for the exterior; but this arrangement had practical disadvantages. First it meant that the oratory would have been slightly smaller than in the original scheme, and secondly there would have been no room for a porter's lodge between it and the church. Borromini tried to get round this difficulty by making another entrance with a porter's lodge to the west of the oratory, but this would have meant having two entrances to guard instead of one. Finally the new arrangement would not have left space between the main entrance and the oratory for the rooms needed for the musicians and for visiting preachers, nor for the gallery facing the altar, which was required for cardinals and other distinguished visitors who might attend the musical performances. In the end Borromini was forced to go back to Maruscelli's arrangement and to put the oratory at the west end of the street front, though he left room for a narrow passage behind the altar to allow circulation on the ground floor and room for musicians' galleries at the upper levels. The plan with two doors, as we can see from a drawing at Windsor, had the advantages of greater symmetry, and in the amended plan the door next to the church is balanced by an almost blank panel, broken only by a small rectangular window; but the more serious consequence of moving the oratory back to the west was that the relation of the exterior to the interior was now quite irrational, since the door in the middle of the façade led not into the centre of the oratory but into the vestibule

under the gallery at the east end. In all these schemes there is a
further weakness, because the visitor automatically takes the facade
to be like that of an ordinary church and, on going into this door,
expects to find himself looking along the main axis of the oratory,
whereas this axis is actually at right angles to his line of approach.
Borromini is honest enough to call attention to the 'deception' as
he calls it, but explains that he was forced into it by circumstances.
As regards the advantages and disadvantages of Borromini's two
schemes, it has been ingeniously pointed out that in the executed
building the façade on the street, though it does not correspond to
what stands immediately behind it, lies on the axis of the two
cloisters and so is related to the whole complex of the building. This
is true for one examining the plan on paper but is not perceptible
to a person actually entering the oratory.

A further problem arose in the matter of fenestration if the oratory
was to be at the end of the south block. Each of the four bays of
the longer sides of the oratory was to have a window at the upper
level, and a difficulty arose in relating them to the bays of the adjoining cloister. The section of the building corresponding to the oratory
consisted of two bays of the cloister arcade and two bays of the staircase. The actual bays were of the same size, but at the corner of
the cloister, that is to say opposite the middle of the oratory, there
occurred a thick pier, which made the spacing irregular, so that,
if the windows were to be evenly spaced, they would not correspond
to the openings opposite them. Borromini solved this problem by
making the middle pier of the oratory, which corresponded to the
corner bay of the cloister, wider than the others, and took advantage
of this by using this pier and the one corresponding to it on the
south side for the pulpit on the south wall and for a niche with the
bust of S. Filippo Neri on the north.

In the arrangement of the cloisters he was seriously hampered
by the existence of the sacristy, which was at a higher level than
the church and had windows placed without any relation to the
cloisters as now planned. He got over the second difficulty by inserting on the outer side of the sacristy walls double windows of which
one half is sham, and he solved the first by placing at the end of
the vestible inside the main entrance a flight of six steps on which
he contrived four seats level with the steps and growing out of them
in elegantly curved forms. Further, the vaulted passage between the
church and the sacristy had been built on two storeys and this fixed
the height of both the ground and first-floor rooms. This was all
right for the south court which contained the grander public rooms,

but it imposed an unsuitable and wasteful height for the first floor of the wing containing the cells of the Fathers, but Borromini adjusted the design so as to include an extra floor in this section and did so with such ingenuity that from the outside the irregularity is not visible.

In the early plans there was to be a floor of cells over the oratory, but in 1638 it was decided to have the library in this position, a change which involved greatly increasing the height of the façade and so making it compete in importance with that of the church. There are unfortunately no drawings of the elevation originally proposed for the façade of this wing before it was decided to heighten it, but as far as we can see from the plan it would have been quite simple, like the wings along the side of the existing building, probably without the use of any order of pilasters.

The addition of a second storey as high as the oratory itself involved a complete change of design, and Borromini reacted to this problem brilliantly [65]. Internally the library had book-cases all round on the level of the floor and a second row on a gallery. Borromini has clearly indicated these two levels on his façade, for the

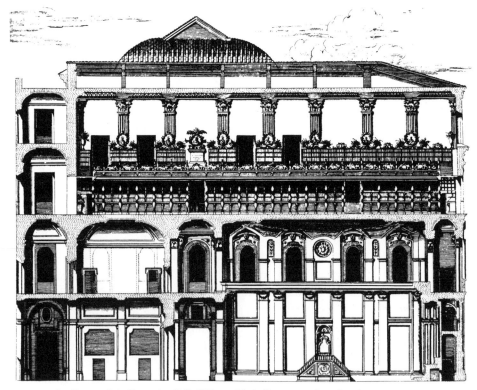

65. Borromini: Oratorio di S. Filippo Neri, Rome, section showing oratory and library, engraving

door in the concave central niche opens at the level of the floor and
the windows are on that of the gallery. Unhappily it was found later
that the west wall of the library, which rested on the vault of the
oratory, was showing signs of weakness, and it was decided to extend
the room to the west end of the site. This involved building up the
top floor to the left of the pilastered façade so that the curves of
the flanking volutes, which were originally meant to stand out
against the sky, are now seen against painted stucco walls and the
carefully thought-out silhouette of the facade is lost. Even in its
original state, however, the relation of the façade of the oratory to
that of the church can never have been completely happy, though
one must remember that the two buildings were meant to be seen
at a fairly sharp angle in the little piazza that the Fathers made in
front of them and not, as at present, across the waste of the Corso
Vittorio Emmanuele. It is interesting to note, however, that later,
at the instigation of Innocent X, Borromini produced a plan to add
another wing to the right of the church which was to be different
in design from that containing the oratory but would have established some sort of symmetry and lessened the present unhappy
relationship of the two façades.

Borromini's description of the façade of the oratory as being like
a man stretching out his arms has already been quoted, but it is
surprising that he – or his spokesman Spada – does not emphasize
the most remarkable feature of the front, namely the fact that it
is built on a continuously curved plan (perhaps in their desire to
rebut accusations of rule-breaking they were not anxious to emphasize the revolutionary features). To this extent it is like the façade
of S. Carlino, but in other respects the two fronts are fundamentally
different. Whereas the facade of S. Carlino is composed mainly of
columns, that of the oratory is articulated entirely with pilasters,
the only columns being the two small ones flanking the door; but
we know from the *Opus* that this was a condition imposed on the
architect by the monks, who were concerned that the façade should
not compete with that of the church, which had to be distinguished
as the most important part of the whole institution. For this reason
they also demanded that the architect should use brick rather than
travertine.

With these conditions in mind Borromini produced a façade of
extraordinary subtlety. Since he could not treat it in a sculptural,
Michelangelesque manner, with effects of relief produced by
columns and decorative sculpture, he went to the opposite extreme
and did everything he could to keep the plane dominant. The

66. Borromini: Oratorio di S. Filippo Neri, Rome, capital on façade

pilasters are shallow, the entablatures and the string courses are light
[66], and the windows project less than is usual with him. That this
was a conscious plan emerges from a remark which he makes in
the *Opus* about the material out of which the front was to be built.
How wonderful it would be, he says, if one could construct a whole
façade out of a single piece of terracotta! But since this was impossible he had taken pains to get bricks which were very thin and regular and laid with so little mortar that the divisions are hardly visible
[67]. For this type of brick he found, he tells us, a model in an ancient
tower outside the Porta del Popolo, and in fact the brickwork of

67. Borromini: Oratorio di S. Filippo Neri, Rome, niche on facade

the oratory can bear comparison with the finest produced by the builders of ancient Rome.

As a result of these careful dispositions the façade of the oratory is entirely different from that of S. Carlino. Instead of being a mass of masonry curving in and out, it has the springiness of a sheet of metal which has been slightly curved under pressure. It is totally unmonumental but is maturely Baroque in that it forces the eye of the observer to move across it along determined lines.

The façade is planned on a single, very slow curve, which is interrupted in the middle section by a projecting convex bay for the door and a concave niche for the balcony to the library. The three middle bays project slightly and are gathered together at the top by a pediment of the type which Borromini had planned to introduce at S. Carlino. Here, however, it is used with greater logic, for at S. Carlino the pediment covers a single bay, whereas at the oratory its three divisions correspond to three bays of the façade, the lines of which are carried up through the field of the pediment itself, as in Vignola's design for the Gesù. It appears at first sight that all the elements of the façade are curved, but the two inner bays of the lower half are actually straight [68]. The purpose of this variation, which is only visible on close inspection, is not clear.

68. Borromini: Oratorio di S. Filippo Neri, Rome, entablatures on façade

Only two complete drawings are known for the façade of the oratory. One at Windsor, which has already been mentioned, is a beautiful fair copy by Borromini himself of the design with two doors [69]. The other, in the Albertina (291), has *pentimenti* which give some information about the architect's intentions. As far as one can decipher the underdrawing it seems to represent the façade as built, but on top Borromini has drawn in, with very forcible strokes, a design in which the wings project in a far sharper curve. This project, which is recorded in one of the engravings in the *Opus architectonicum* and may possibly have been drawn – or redrawn – specially for it late in Borromini's career, would perhaps have been more

69. Borromini: Oratorio di S. Filippo Neri, Rome, drawing for façade

dramatic, but it is hard to see how the façade could have been integrated into the whole front.

As it stands the decoration of the façade of the oratory is very simple. The hoods of the windows and niches are of travertine, but

96    their surrounds are of brick; the mouldings are of travertine, but the pilasters themselves are of brick, except for their capitals, which include stars and lilies [66]. The only points of richness occur in

70. Borromini: Oratorio di S. Filippo Neri, Rome, central balcony

the central bay. The door has travertine columns and a pediment broken in an unusual way, and the window above it has a curved hood reminiscent of the Palazzo Barberini window but with gentler curves, supported by the two Michelangelesque consoles which were analysed in Chapter 2. The balcony [70] has balusters of the type used in the cloister of S. Carlino, and the niche is decorated with coffering like that in the half-domes of the church. Borromini's one outburst occurs in the decoration of the door leading on to the balcony from the library. Its jambs are supported by palms and its

71. Borromini: Oratorio di S. Filippo Neri, Rome, project for façade, engraving

pediment is composed of two scrolls which are joined by a swag of laurel leaves, behind which is a palmette of almost Attic elegance, a motif which Borromini was to use again in his later work.

Borromini tells us, however, that this simplicity was imposed on him by the Fathers, and the plate in the *Opus architectonicum* just mentioned shows the project which he was forced to abandon [71]. Architecturally the only important difference is that the first scheme shows columns, not over the whole façade but on the middle three bays of the upper storey, an arrangement which would have made for a top-heavy effect. The more obvious differences concern the sculptural decoration. The skyline of the façade was to have supported pedestals on which were stars, olive branches, palms, lilies, and fleurs-de-lys. The Windsor drawing, which is closely related to this engraving and also shows columns on the middle sections of the upper storey, has flaming hearts and stars. The window over the central door was to have had swags of laurel leaves hanging from the consoles, and the door itself was to have been much more elaborate. It was to have had twisted columns with elaborate capitals composed of lotus leaves and cherubs' heads, and a superstructure in which the triangle of the pediment was lifted up and supported on two scrolls, an arrangement which was widely exploited by later Baroque architects all over Europe but which seems to have been used here for the first time. It can be regarded as a development from Michelangelo, who in the upper windows in the courtyard of the Palazzo Farnese took the revolutionary step of separating the hoods from the windows themselves and supporting them on capitals with guttae. The sculptural decoration of the door was to have been much more elaborate and would have included palms, lilies, stars, a crown, a flaming heart and a winged cherub's head.

Almost all the decorative elements in the abandoned design and on the actual building are symbolical. The flaming hearts and the lilies – with which the fleurs-de-lys are interchangeable – are favourite symbols of S. Filippo Neri; the crown and the palms are associated with eternal life, though, taken in conjunction with the cherubs' heads and the Solomonic columns, the palms may contain an allusion to the Holy of Holies in the Temple of Solomon. The star has eight points and cannot, therefore, be the star of David, which has six. It probably has a quite different significance, because Borromini, who uses it in the decoration of the library, tells us that it was there a symbol of the Fathers of the church, who were said to shine like the stars in the firmament.

The general layout of the buildings of the Oratory is set by the two cloisters. As has already been said, the design of these was conditioned by the presence of the sacristy which prevented Borromini from making them completely symmetrical because of the placing of the windows, which made it impossible for the architect to continue the order of pilasters along this side. In the first cloister he simply carried on the string course over the lower order of arches and made it rise above the line of the windows, producing a not altogether satisfactory effect. In the second cloister he used a small order of Ionic pilasters at the south and, as the rooms along the

north side of the sacristy were of one storey only, there was no problem of fenestration. In the 1870s, however, the three southern bays
of this cloister were cut off and filled with a wing the height of those
occupying the other three sides, and the order of giant pilasters was
continued along it. This addition completely changed the character
of the cloister, making it a square of five bays each way, as opposed
to a rectangle of five by eight bays, and cutting off much of the light
from the south. In the middle of the top floor on the south face
of the sacristy Borromini put a window like those inserted by a follower of Michelangelo in the middle of the Capitoline Palaces, but
this was destroyed in the 1920s. The giant order which he used in
the cloisters was, as he tells us, also taken from these palaces, but
with the difference that here they enclose two arcades, whereas on
the Capitol both floors have flat trabeations.

The short west side of the first cloister is occupied by the staircase,
which follows the normal Roman pattern of a single flight doubling
back on itself, but with the difference that the upper stage opens
up into a wide vault covering both flights, so that the visitor finds
himself moving from a narrow dark space into a zone that is wider
and better lit. Borromini speaks of this arrangement as being of his
own invention, and he tells us that he also used it in the Palazzo
di Spagna. It appears in fact to be a novelty in Roman architecture,
but it was not unknown in northern Italy and appears in the treatises
of both Palladio and Scamozzi.

From the cloister the visitor enters the staircase through a square
bay supported on four granite columns which already belonged to
the Fathers, but as they were slightly too short, Borromini inserted
a section at the bottom, decorated with lotus leaves, so that, as he
says, they appear to be growing out of the plants. He might have
added that this was a well-known device in works of ancient architecture which he certainly knew, such as the vine-columns of St
Peter's, the columns in the choir of S. Prassede, and another
example which he himself copied from the Codex Coner. Further,
it had been imitated in the Baldacchino of St Peter's, with the design
of which he himself was connected.

The most important room in the interior of the building is the
oratory itself, of which the placing and general disposition have
already been discussed. Borromini was concerned with the problem
of vaulting such a wide space, and he tells us that he inserted
pilasters at the corners to add support to carry the load. This device
he borrowed from ancient buildings, of which he quotes Hadrian's
Villa, the Baths of Diocletian and one which had recently been exca-

vated by the Marchese del Bufalo in his vigna near the hospital of S. Giovanni in Laterano. This arrangement involved cutting off the corners of the room, as had already been done in the refectory of S. Carlino. The walls are articulated by Ionic pilasters which are continued above the entablature by flat pilaster bands. The vault itself is a low, coved structure divided by applied ribs which recall Gothic vaulting but do not in fact perform any structural function. In arrangement they are also like those which divide the vault of Mantegna's Camera degli Sposi in the Castello di S. Giorgio at Mantua, but it is unlikely that there is any direct connection between the two works. Here the 'ribs' do not run right across the vault but abut on an oval panel in the middle which contained a painting of the Coronation of the Virgin by Romanelli, now replaced by a less happy work. The galleries for the musicians and the distinguished visitors have balustrades like that on the balcony of the façade and gilt-bronze grilles with stars, fleurs-de-lys, and palmettes. For occasions when the audience was exceptionally large Borromini contrived an overflow room under the oratory itself, which could be reached by a small spiral staircase in the north-west corner of the room and to which the music penetrated through two grilles in the floor of the oratory.

The oratory is approached by three doors. The one for the public in the middle of the façade has already been discussed, but the other two are equally remarkable. That in the north wall was designed for the use of the Fathers and has richly moulded jambs and an unusual covering in which, as on the projected door for the façade, the pediment has been lifted up from the door itself, but here it is carried by a sort of broken architrave instead of by scrolls. The most spectacular of the doors, however, is that leading into the oratory from the vestibule adjoining the main entrance to the building [72]. Here the jambs stand out in mouldings of a richness which even Borromini himself never surpassed and which show how far he could enlarge on the lessons that he had learnt from Michelangelo. The pediment is again lifted, this time on an architrave broken into complicated curves and enclosing a medallion containing the bust of S. Filippo Neri, supported by winged cherubs' heads, over which is a flaming heart. Unfortunately the vestibule in which the door stands is now so dark that it is difficult to appreciate the richness of the design of the door. Borromini insists on the fact that he arranged for as much light as possible to be admitted through the adjacent room, but recent alterations have destroyed the effect which he intended.

*Scala di Palmi Romani*

72. Borromini: Oratorio di S. Filippo Neri, Rome, door to oratory, engraving

73. Borromini: Oratorio di S. Filippo Neri, Rome,
monument to Cardinal Baronius

Of the lesser rooms in the interior the most interesting are the
library [65], the refectory and the Sala di Ricreazione. The library,
unfortunately, lost its true proportions when it was extended, and
it is now mainly notable for its elegant galleries and bookshelves.
Borromini tells us that he at first planned to have the galleries supported on columns, but that he found that they would be too bulky
and would hide the books. He therefore followed the advice of a
Florentine friend, the architect Filippo Arigucci, who suggested
that he should instead use wooden balusters, which could be made
much lighter. As a model he quoted the tomb of a Grand Duke
of Tuscany. This reference is somewhat puzzling, as none of the
tombs of the Grand Dukes of the Cappella dei Principi in S.
Lorenzo has any features of this kind, and it is more likely that Arri-
gucci was referring to one of the temporary structures put up in
the church itself for the obsequies of the Grand Dukes, though
nothing precisely similar is to be found in surviving drawings or
engravings. The effect is indeed very elegant and the balusters har-
monize perfectly with the light rail which Borromini placed round
the gallery and in which he incorporated the panels from the old
library, which named the different sections under which the books
were classed. He also re-used much of the fine walnut from the old
bookshelves. Over the door leading on to the balcony and opposite
the visitor as he comes into the room is a bust of Cardinal Baronius
[73], set in a wreath of laurel with stars below, lilies at the sides
and palms above. The base contains an inscription, above which
runs a narrow frieze of fleurs-de-lys, and below it is a bas-relief like
a trophy of arms but composed of a papal tiara, a cardinal's hat,
a bishop's mitre, a crozier and a processional cross, the symbols of
the church of which Baronius was one of the great historians.

The refectory and the Sala di Ricreazione lie one above the other
in an awkwardly shaped area in the north-east corner of the site,
behind the apse of the church. Maruscelli had planned a rectangular
refectory, with its long axis running across that of the church, but
Borromini moved it further west and turned its axis so that it ran
parallel with the cloister. This made it more easily accessible and
left a convenient room for the *lavamano*, where the Fathers washed
before meals, between the staircase and the refectory itself. As an
example of the architect's attention to detail it is interesting to note
that he designed a cupboard with divisions in which the Fathers
could keep their napkins. He originally planned the refectory as a
long rectangle with the corners cut off, like the oratory, but later
changed its form and that of the Sala di Ricreazione to ovals. He

chose this form partly, no doubt, because the shape appealed to him, but primarily for practical reasons. It enabled him to make the best use of the available space and, as he himself tells us, it was more convenient for the monks who at their meals were accustomed to engage in discussion on matters of theology and were able to do so more easily in an oval room than if they sat side by side in straight rows.

Both the refectory and the Sala di Ricreazione have lost much of their character through being adapted to other uses, but it is still possible to enjoy the most remarkable feature of the Sala di Ricreazione, the fireplace [74]. This is a huge structure, nearly eighteen feet long. Apart from the top, which is of stucco, the whole fireplace is of marble, the overmantel being cut from a single block which

74. Borromini: Oratorio di S. Filippo Neri, Rome,
**Sala di Ricreazione**, fireplace

Borromini discovered while digging the foundations of the oratory. The marble is white with some streaks of greenish grey and
of a very coarse grain, which gives it a curious luminosity through
the fact that individual crystals glitter in the light. It is designed
like a tent, forming a convex oval which protrudes into the room
and plays against the concave wall. The fringe of the tent, which
hangs down over the opening for the fire, has been converted by
Borromini into a Doric frieze, in which the metopes are decorated
with the Oratorian symbols: stars, flaming hearts [75], and lilies.
From it hangs a line of little tassels. At the sides the 'tent' disappears
into reentrant curves ornamented with fluted panels, of which the
origins in late Roman column designs have been discussed in
Chapter 2. In a reproduction the fireplace looks rather trivial and

75. Borromini: Oratorio di S. Filippo Neri, Rome,
Sala di Ricreazione, fireplace, detail

fussy, but its scale and the beauty of the marble save it from these
failings and it must be judged one of Borromini's grandest inventions in the way of room furniture.

An equally beautiful piece of furniture, this time on a very small scale, is the *lavamano* which stands in the vestibule to the refectory [76]. This is in the form of a tulip, of which four petals stand up

76. Borromini: Oratorio di S. Filippo Neri, Rome, *lavamano*

in the middle and four more are spread out to hold the water. This once came out of taps in the shape of birds and bees, but these have now disappeared. The base of the *lavamano* is more like a cluster of late Gothic pillars than anything in the repertory of classical architecture. It may be a late reminiscence of the bases of the piers in Milan cathedral.

The last section of the oratory to be erected was the west wing ending with the clock-tower facing the Piazza di Monte Giordano, which was put up in 1647–9. The wing itself, which contains the cells of the Fathers, is of no great interest architecturally, but the

clock-tower has novel features [77]. Internally it is an oval of the
same form as the dome of S. Carlino, but the outer shell is more
complex. The two shorter sides follow the oval of the interior,
though with a slightly flattened curve, but the other two consist of
concave bays, the form of which changes as it rises. At the lower
stage it consists of two piers projecting at angles of 45° and flanking
a middle straight section, but at the top the bay is a continuous concave curve. Borromini makes the transition from one form to the
other by means of a recessed panel which covers the change in the
plane of the main wall and leads the eye from one stage to the other.
He was to use the same device, even more ingeniously concealed,
in the dome of S. Ivo. As Borromini originally designed it, the
decoration of the clock-tower was to contain the same symbols as
the façade of the oratory. The bells were to have been suspended

77. Borromini: Piazza di Monte Giordano with clock-tower
and Palazzo di Spirito Santo, Rome, engraving

from an iron construction composed of fleurs-de-lys and stars, and
the face of the clock was to have had in the centre a flaming heart
pierced by an arrow with a fleur-de-lys head, which pointed to the
hours.

At the same time as he was engaged on the oratory Borromini received one of his few commissions for a work outside Rome. Martinelli tells us that Cardinal Ascanio Filomarino, archbishop of
Naples, a protégé of Urban VIII and a keen patron of the arts, was
so much impressed by S. Carlino that he invited Borromini to design

for him an altar [78] for his family chapel in the church of SS. Apostoli in Naples, recently built for the Theatines on the designs of Fabrizio Grimaldi. The exact date of the commission is not known, but Filomarino was negotiating with the Theatines in 1635 for permission to erect the altar in their church and one of the mosaics which it contains is dated that year. Work continued on it for a long period and payments to one of the sculptors are recorded in 1647.

It is often said that it was made entirely in Rome, and the conclusion has been drawn from this that Borromini never visited Naples and never saw the place where the altar was to be erected. However, the altar fits the transept of the SS. Apostoli so harmoniously that it seems unthinkable that it should have been designed by someone who had not actually seen the setting in which it was to be placed. Fortunately the payments show that much of the sculpture was carried out in Naples, and there is other evidence to show that Borromini visited the city. Among Spada's papers in the Vatican there is a note in which Borromini gives a description of the dome of the Cappella del Tesoro in the cathedral at Naples, in particular of the way in which it is lit, which could only be based on actual observation. It would in any case be completely out of character for Borromini to produce a work without knowing the setting for which it was destined, the architecture of the church in which it was to stand, the lighting and all the other pre-existing factors which were always for him the starting-point for any design.

A number of artists were involved in the execution of the altar. The five main panels are copies in mosaic by Giovanni Battista Calandra after paintings by Guido Reni which, according to tradition, belonged to the Cardinal. The two oval portraits which are placed, as if hung on ribbons, one on each side of the altar, are also by Calandra, but the authors of the originals are unknown (the traditional attributions to Pietro da Cortona and the French artist Valentin are as unconvincing as one to Reni recently proposed). The relief of putti over the mensa is by the Flemish sculptor François Duquesnoy, a close friend of Poussin, of whom Filomarino was also a patron, and Giuliano Finelli is responsible for the lions supporting it and for the relief between them representing the sacrifice of Isaac. The columns and capitals are due to Lorenzo Chiani, Domenico Tavolacci and the Neapolitan Francesco Mezzetti.

The altar consists of three bays, of which the two side ones project on a slightly concave curve. Four composite columns support an entablature which breaks forward strongly over them, and the two central columns are joined by a pediment of the form used by Borro-

78. Borromini: SS. Apostoli, Naples, Filomarino altar, begun *c.* 1635

mini on the façade of the oratory. The top of the altar is decorated with the kind of ornaments which the architect had intended for the oratory but which had been banned by the Fathers. In the middle is a feature composed of the volutes of an Ionic capital extended to right and left by scrolls and carrying the Filomarino arms. Over the side bays are Porta Pia volute motifs supporting icosahedra – solids with twenty faces each an equilateral triangle – one of the regular solids out of which Plato constructs the universe in the *Timaeus*. Over the end columns are vases with flowers. Over the mensa runs a broad band decorated with high reliefs incorporating heraldic and floral motifs. The front of the mensa is a kind of Doric frieze – like that on the fireplace in the Oratory – in which the metopes are filled alternately with circular shields and the symbols of the Evangelists, and the altar-rails are of the usual Borrominesque form. Like the whole altar itself, they are executed in very fine white Carrara marble.

Though the general form of the altar is like that of the façade of the oratory, it is altogether different in character. This is one of the very few occasions when Borromini worked in rich materials, and he has adapted his style to the medium. The whole altar has a richness of architectural forms which is the counterpart of the luxurious material. The mouldings of the entablature are deep and throw heavy shadows; the decorative sculpture is mainly in high relief and rich in naturalistic detail, and the composite capitals are as magnificent as those that Borromini designed for the Baldacchino of St Peter's. The model in this case is probably a capital engraved by Montano (*Li cinque libri di architettura*, Book I, Pl. 23), and for the fluting he turned to the same source and used the model which he had already followed in the fireplace at the oratory and, incidentally, in the side-chapels of S. Carlino. Presumably to make the capitals of the columns even more conspicuous, he has treated the half-pilasters which flank them in a much simpler manner, replacing the acanthus with a simple grooved motif almost like a Doric triglyph.

In the Filomarino altar Borromini primarily concerned himself with decorative problems, and in the oratory he had been mainly occupied with problems of planning, conditioned by the site and the requirements of the Fathers, and had had little opportunity of displaying the inventiveness in spatial designs which was so marked in S. Carlino, but in the next major work, the church of S. Ivo della Sapienza, he returned to the ideas which he had worked out in his first church and produced what is probably his most brilliant invention in terms of space and mass.

# S. Ivo della Sapienza
# and S. Maria dei Sette Dolori

In 1632, on the recommendation of Bernini and at the instance of Urban VIII, Borromini was appointed to the post of architect to the Archiginnasio – later the University – of Rome, called the Sapienza [79], one of the only two public posts that he ever held. A great part of the buildings had been erected in the later sixteenth century by Pirro Ligorio and Giacomo della Porta under Pius IV and his successors, but work had stopped under Paul V and, though the long court with its two superimposed arcades was nearly finished, the library, the church and the east façade behind it remained to be built, and the west façade was incomplete.

Borromini made designs for finishing and indeed basically altering the west façade [80], but they were never carried out. Giacomo della Porta had designed a front with the ground floor broken only by a central door. Borromini proposed to make the façade less fortress-like by rusticating the masonry and replacing the single door with two larger ones through which the visitor would have had vistas down the two long cloisters. In addition he proposed to lighten the effect of della Porta's squat towers, of which only one was actually built, by adding to them a second floor consisting of an open *tempietto* with concave sides. The towers must have been designed during the pontificate of Innocent X, as the engravings show them crowned with the Pamphili dove.

Borromini's main concern, however, was the building of the church. The foundation stone was laid in January 1643 and the structure was finished by 1648, when the dome was being covered with lead. The cross and globe on the top of the lantern were being gilded in 1652. After that there was a considerable interval, and the decoration of the interior was not begun till 1659. The floor was laid in 1660 and the church was consecrated in the same year.

The church [81] was to fill the space at the end of the court and so would face the visitor as he entered the building. In planning

80. Borromini: The Sapienza, Rome, entrance façade, engraving

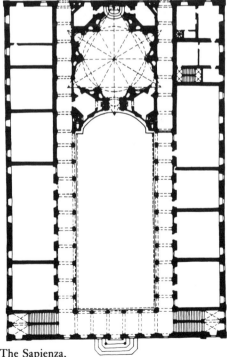

81. Borromini: The Sapienza,
Rome, plan, engraving

it Borromini was much restricted by the existing buildings. The cloisters on either side of the court were already laid out and were to be continued through to the east end of the site, and della Porta had also begun the concave bay which closes the court. The space left was almost square and della Porta had planned a circular church with very small side-chapels, which would have satisfied practical needs but would have lacked all architectural character. Within this space, however, Borromini evolved a plan of the most startling originality. The liturgical function of a centralized plan as a suitable setting for the contemplation of the Sacrament has already been mentioned in connection with S. Carlino, but in S. Ivo it has a further significance in that it is also a convenient plan for the preaching and hearing of sermons, to which the University, which was dominated by its theological faculty, attached great importance. Moreover the actual form of the vault, which, as has often been pointed out, is a sort of tent, may well be intended to echo on a large scale the little tent-like silk covering, which was – and still often is – placed over the tabernacle containing the Sacrament.

The general design is of extreme ingenuity, and in it Borromini brought to full maturity the ideas with which he had been experimenting at S. Carlino and the Oratory. The plan [83] is based on two equilateral triangles which interpenetrate to form a six-pointed star on the outer periphery and a regular hexagon as the central space. The church itself is composed of this hexagon, surrounded by three pairs of alternating bays. One type of bay is formed by drawing a semi-circle with one of the sides of the hexagon as diameter. The other bays are more complicated in form. Their sides are straight and lie along the outlines of the star, but they end in a curved section which is convex inwards and is an arc of a circle drawn with its centre at the point of the star and with the same radius as the semi-circular bays. Every element therefore of this complex pattern is derived from the first geometrical skeleton, with as much precision as at S. Carlino and with the added factor that in S. Ivo the plan is completely centralized and is symmetrical about six axes. The effect of movement established by this plan is most easily appreciated in a view looking up into the dome [82], in which the eye is carried round the line of the entablature in a ceaseless swing, moving from the simple concavity of one bay to the broken and more angular form of the next. Never perhaps did the Baroque ideal of movement attain more complete and perfect expression.

We know from several sources – from Martinelli, from an engraving in the *Opera* and from a passage in the brief introduction to

82 and 83. Borromini:
S. Ivo della Sapienza, Rome,
interior of dome,
and diagram of plan

it, and from one of Borromini's drawings – that the plan was originally intended to symbolize the bee of the Barberini family, the head, body and four wings corresponding to the six bays of the church, but it seems certain that the architect must also have had in mind the idea that the six-pointed star is the star of David, the accepted symbol of wisdom, and therefore peculiarly appropriate to the church of the Sapienza.

There are no precise precedents for this type of plan among buildings of the sixteenth century. Ascanio Vittozzi had taken a triangle as the basis for the plan of SS. Trinità in Turin (begun in 1598), but the resultant plan is so much simpler than that of S. Ivo that the parallel is hardly relevant; a small sketch also exists by Peruzzi for a hexagonal building with alternately semi-circular and triangular bays, though it is not known whether it is an original invention of his own or a drawing after an ancient building. In any case it is unlikely that Borromini knew Peruzzi's sketch, and his own plan is far bolder and far more sophisticated. In his treatment of the vaulting he was no doubt inspired by ancient examples such as the Serapeum at Hadrian's Villa which was much studied in the seventeenth century.

Borromini's treatment of the elevation of the interior is very different from that which he used at S. Carlino. There the three zones of walls, pendentives and dome are organized on quite different principles, but at S. Ivo [84] Borromini continues the ground plan right up the full height of the church, making the dome by the simple process of shrinking the plan up to the base of the lantern, almost as if it was a tent, as Martinelli points out. This continuity is made possible by the fact that at the lower stage Borromini articulates his walls with pilasters and not columns, so that he establishes sharp edges for the bays which can be carried up into the vault and gathered together at the level of the lantern. The fact that he uses no columns does not, however, mean that the walls are entirely treated in planes. They are, on the contrary, broken up by a variety of niches which carve space out of them [84, 85]. One of the semi-circular bays houses the High Altar, which will be considered in a moment, but the other two contain doors which lead to the two small rooms, on either side of the entrance. The doors are composed of two openings at right angles to each other in a niche covered by a half-dome, a very unusual arrangement which Borromini probably took from the early Christian church of S. Lorenzo in Milan, which had been restored in the sixteenth century by Martino Bassi. On each side there is a smaller niche inserted between a pair of

84. Borromini: S. Ivo della Sapienza, Rome, section, engraving

pilasters, but the upper zone of the walls in these bays is unbroken, save by the two string courses which run all round the church, seeming to pass behind the pilasters. The other three bays are composed in a quite different way. On the lower level the convex central panel has a niche larger than those in the semi-circular bays and forming a contrast of concave and convex, like that in the central bay of the façade of the Oratory but in stronger form. At the upper level the

85. Borromini: S. Ivo della Sapienza, Rome, interior

side sections have rectangular panels like their neighbours in the semi-circular bays, but the middle section contains a gallery. The opening of this now ends in a flat trabeation with its corners cut off by little quadrants, but, as we know from an eighteenth-century drawing, it was originally enclosed under a round-headed arch below its present flat top. It also originally had a balustrade of the familiar Borrominesque type.

This description of the structure of the church does not take into account certain subtle variations which Borromini introduces and which are not apparent at first sight. The first is that his curved bays are slightly more than semi-circles; in the altar bay, for instance, the true diameter runs along the upper step, not along the lower one which joins the bases of the pilasters. The result is that the angle made by the two sections of the entablature which meet

86. Borromini: S. Ivo della Sapienza, Rome, detail of entablature

at this point is acute, only very slightly but enough to produce the effect that the corners of the entablature are pressing in towards the centre of the church [86].

The deviation in the dome is more subtle and harder to detect. In the semi-circular bays the vault rises continuously, always on the same plan, but in the other bays, whereas the entablature has the form straight–convex–straight of the wall below it, when the vault reaches the ring round the lantern it has turned into a simple concave curve, like its neighbours, and so can form part of the ring [87]. Borromini deceives the eye, because the spring of the vault actually consists of three straight elements, but the fact is scarcely visible because the side sections are very narrow and the middle is occupied by the open space of the window which does not define any plane. At the top of the window Borromini gathers these three

87. Borromini: S. Ivo della Sapienza, Rome, detail of dome

straight elements into a single concave curve which he continues up to the ring round the lantern.

The symbolism which underlies the plan is continued in the decoration. This was not carried out till the pontificate of Alexander VII and it contains many references to the Chigi arms. The crowned *monti* with stars fill alternate panels of the dome and they appear again, alternating with the della Rovere oak branches, which the Chigi were allowed by Julius II to quarter in their arms, round the base of the lantern, and the acorns alone also appear in the capitals of the pilasters. Allusions to the Chigi arms are continued in the narrow sections of the dome which are decorated with stars, but here they do not have a monopoly of the symbolism because they are made to alternate with the six-pointed star of David, and so we are brought back to the theme of the Temple. This in fact appears in other parts of the decoration. The beautifully crisp palms over the doors leading to the side-chapels probably refer to eternal life rather than the Temple, since they are combined with crowns, but on the dome we find them accompanied by the winged cherubs' heads which form a ring below the lantern, and the architect's intention becomes even clearer from a preliminary drawing in which he uses whole palm-trees instead of leaves, a more explicit allusion to the Holy of Holies.

The whole interior of the church was to have been a symbol of wisdom. According to the inscription on one of the drawings for the first project of the church, there were to have been seven columns behind the High Altar symbolizing the Seven Pillars of Wisdom mentioned in the Old Testament, and the body of the church was to have been a stage on which the manifestations of the wisdom of the New Testament were to have been enacted, through the theme of Pentecost; for the dove of the Holy Ghost was to have been depicted in the top of the lantern, and the twelve apostles were to have appeared in the twelve main niches round the walls of the nave, if we are to accept the evidence of the early eighteenth-century plates of the *Opera*. There are parallels for this form of depicting the subject of Pentecost in some early medieval churches, for instance, St Mark's, Venice.

One of the most puzzling features of the church is the design of the marble pavement, which is based on an octagon in spite of the fact that the church is hexagonal. Borromini apparently decided at an early stage to use the commonest type of marble unit which consists of two rhomboidal sections, one white, one grey, put together so that their longest side is in common and all the angles are of 45° or 135°. He put forward two alternative ways of using this unit, one with all the slabs running parallel across the whole area of the floor, the other with the units radiating from the centre of the floor. The first was rejected, presumably because the pattern would have run counter to the emphatically centralized design of the church, but the choice of the second led to the awkward fact that the eight sections into which the floor was broken up did not correspond to the six bays of the walls, with the result that the lines along which the sections join strike the periphery at points which do not correspond to the articulation of the wall. In the execution of the floor Borromini minimized the clumsiness of the effect by putting straight lines of grey marble across the openings to the six main bays of the church and paving these bays with slabs set parallel with each other, but it remains true that when the whole floor is visible, as it was certainly intended to be, the radial lines separating the different sections strike the hexagon at points on the sides and not at the corners.

The reason why Borromini chose to use this particular design is not clear, because, if he had used a unit in which the angles were 30° and 150°, he could have divided his floor radially into six sections. It has been suggested that he chose not to use a sixfold division because, owing to the subtle changes which he had introduced into the plan of the church, there would have been slight irregularities in the sides of the hexagonal periphery, but this argument does not seem convincing, because it would have been quite easy to adjust the laying of the slabs so as to conceal the variations. An alternative explanation is economy, because, though it would not have been technically difficult to cut the slabs to angles of 30° and 150° degrees, this was not the form normally used in Rome at the time, and would no doubt have cost more than using the standard unit.

In 1859 the interior of S. Ivo was grievously 'restored'. The walls were covered with sham painted marble of extreme coarseness; the galleries were altered in the way already described; and the bay containing the High Altar was radically changed. Borromini had himself hesitated about the form of this bay. A preliminary drawing – referred to above – shows that he at first intended to have behind the altar a semi-circular row of columns, almost like the apse of Palladio's Redentore in small. This project he abandoned for one with a solid backing for the altar but with light coming in from a window above. The commission for the altarpiece was given to Pietro da Cortona but was left unfinished at his death in 1669 and only completed by a member of his studio in 1683, when a new setting for it was prepared by Giovanni Battista Contini. In the restoration of 1859 the whole bay was altered; the existing coffered arch was introduced, and the large outside window on the east façade was blocked up. It is therefore almost impossible to estimate the effect of this crucially important feature of the church as it was built by Borromini.

Recently the interior of the church has again been restored and the worst of the nineteenth-century alterations have been removed. The false marbling has gone and the walls and dome are now almost white, so that it is possible again to see Borromini's real intentions. But, though the disappearance of the nineteenth-century decorations is an immense advantage, certain doubts still remain. Did

Borromini really intend the whole interior to be as uniformly white
as it is today? The evidence revealed at the time of the restoration was
not conclusive, because the nineteenth-century paint and varnish
had largely destroyed what remained underneath, but it seemed to
indicate that originally the walls might have been modulated in
shades of off-white and pale grey. One may also hesitate about the
gilding of the stars on the dome. The records do not show any
payments for their being gilded, whereas this is recorded for the
panel of the Holy Ghost in the top of the lantern; but now that
they are white, they seem to disappear into the field of the dome
more than one would expect. It is possible that this may be due
to the very strong light which now floods the church, for there is
reason to think that originally the windows were more heavily leaded
and therefore would have let in less light. The fact remains, however, that, whereas on the walls modulations of tone are created by
the mouldings which cast blue-grey shadows, in the dome the relief
is low and the light so even that no such effect occurs. One may
also wonder whether Borromini would have left the white walls and
dome relieved by only two points of gilding, the two grilles in the
balconies, though of course he probably intended to use gold in the
decoration round the High Altar. The two grilles would stand out
less awkwardly in isolation if their gold was repeated in, say, the
palms and crown in the half-domes over the doors to the sacristies.

The exterior [79] is as remarkable as the interior. The lower part
of the interior is concealed behind the exedra, for which Borromini
followed Giacomo della Porta's ground-plan, though he designed
an unusual door with a double pediment, which was not executed.
Above the exedra rises what appears to be a drum, but, as in the
case of S. Carlino, Borromini has followed the Lombard tradition
of enveloping the actual cupola in a cylinder of masonry to take the
lateral thrust. In this case this arrangement was almost forced on
him, because owing to the narrowness of the site he had no room
to add vaulted chapels or buttresses to perform this function. The
'drum' does not precisely express the form of the dome, because
it consists in plan of six lobes, all convex, and does not reflect the
alternations of bays in the interior. This again was probably done
in order to increase the mass of masonry to take the thrust. It is
interesting to notice that while the dome was in building some critics
expressed doubts about its solidity and a note exists in Borromini's
hand in which he recalls the undertaking usually given by architects
at the time to take responsibility for any weakness which might
appear in their buildings for a period of fifteen years, and he proudly

accepts this responsibility for his dome. In fact no cracks appeared, although in the nineteenth century some extra support was added to the bay containing the High Altar.

Over the drum is a stepped zone which, like the upper part of the dome of S. Carlino, recalls the Pantheon; but here it is fully exposed to view and forms an important part of the whole design. The contour of this zone is slightly convex, echoing the curve of the dome inside it, and Borromini has introduced a typical contrast

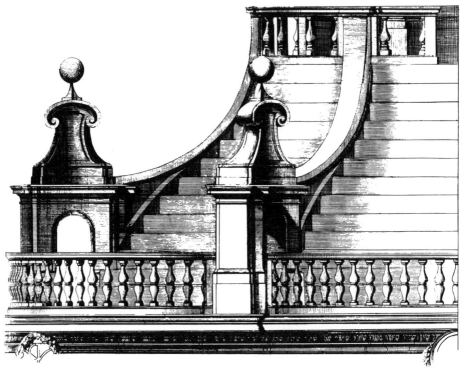

88. Borromini: S. Ivo della Sapienza, Rome, lower part of dome, engraving

by making the low buttresses which run along it concave [88]. They end, it will be noticed, in piers having the form of the Porta Pia Ionic motif.

Above this stepped zone is the lantern composed in its lower stage of a rotunda, which, as been said, recalls the circular temple at Baalbek and also a drawing by Montanus [29, 30]. This leads to the most fanciful feature of all, the spiral ramp, twisting round the internal cone of the lantern and leading up to the climax of the whole building, the wrought-iron flame-like structure which supports a globe and a cross.

Even the more fantastic parts of the dome are related to a strict
geometrical scheme. Borromini's original drawing (Albertina 509)
and the engraved plan of the stepped dome [89] show that the steps
are not, as one might at first expect, a series of concentric circles,
but that they are arcs of circles of the same radius, drawn from

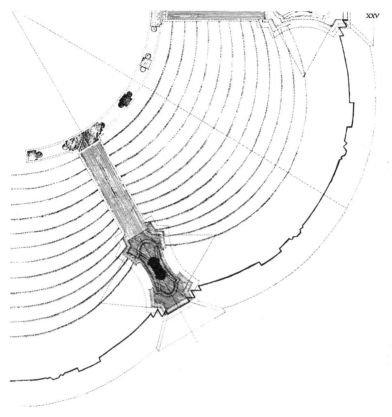

89. Borromini: S. Ivo della Sapienza, Rome, plan of stepped dome, engraving

centres which are moved back by the width of a step for each successive circle. Further, the lines of the Porta Pia motif all meet on the
circumference of the lowest step. At the higher level all the elements
of the concave bays of the lantern are formed by arcs of circles drawn
from centres on the outer perimeter of the whole lantern, and the
spiral of the lantern consists of two series of concentric semi-circles.

The evidence for these geometrical constructions is to be found
in the engravings which illustrate the *Opera*, and it has sometimes
been suggested that they represent a system imposed on the plans by
the engraver and that they do not correspond to Borromini's inten-

tions. Fortunately, however, the architect's original drawing for the stepped roof exists in the Albertina, and it proves beyond doubt that Borromini actually constructed his design by the method indicated above, because it is still possible to see the holes which the architect made as he stuck the leg of the compasses into the paper. The engraver has followed his method exactly, though he has increased the scale to more than double that of the original.

The similarity of the lantern of S. Ivo to the ancient ziggurats of Mesopotamia has often been pointed out, and it is more than likely that Borromini knew engravings, such as one by Martin van Heemskerk, which show the Tower of Babel in this form. By a curious twist, however, the tower, which started as a symbol of human folly, later came to be used to represent the exactly opposite idea, and the confusion of tongues associated with Babel was transformed into the knowledge of tongues given to the Apostles at Pentecost, as represented in the interior of the church. The Tower of Babel becomes the *turris sapientiae*, the tower of wisdom, and was even used by Martin van Heemskerk to represent the light-giving pharos of Alexandria, an obvious symbol of wisdom. It also occurs as a symbol for the wisdom of Solomon in a fifteenth-century painting by Butinone (in the National Gallery of Scotland), in which the youthful Christ arguing with the doctors in the Temple is shown on a spiral structure like the lantern of S. Ivo.

The top of the whole structure is composed of a series of symbols taken from the *Iconologia* of Cesare Ripa, first published in 1593 (first illustrated edition 1603), and a favourite source for seventeenth-century artists. The wrought-iron, flame-like structure represents the desire for knowledge, inspired by intellect; and the flaming torches round the base of the lantern stand for knowledge itself.

Heraldic symbolism is continued on the exterior of the church in the huge three-dimensional *monti* flanking the drum, which stand over the spiral staircases leading to the dome, and in the eight-pointed stars in the openings of the balustrade between them. In the cornice below the stepped dome Borromini uses again a device which he had introduced in the decoration of S. Lucia in Selci and transforms the egg-and-dart moulding so that the eggs are cherubs' heads and the tongues are formed by their wings [12].

Borromini's other additions to the Sapienza are of a less spectacular kind. On the east façade he was able to carry out the design which he had planned for the west, setting two doors on the axes of the cloisters and putting over them large windows with slightly curved

90. Borromini: S. Ivo della Sapienza, Rome, view from east

pediments of which the lower lines are interrupted by the arches of the windows [90]. The pediments were originally to have been supported by herms, but in the event these were replaced by Michelangelesque consoles.

The sections of the facade over the doors are raised a storey higher than the rest of the front by attics which run in a semi-circle back to the middle point of the drum, so that its concavity forms a strong contrast to the convexity of the dome itself. Along the top of the façade runs a parapet with a sort of wave pattern, a design very unusual in Italy and more reminiscent of the type of balustrade used by François Mansart, for instance in the staircase in the château of Maisons.

The right-hand wing encloses the library built under Alexander VII and by him named the Alessandrina. Its lines are more severe than those of the Vallicelliana at the Oratory and the only display of fancy is to be found in the ornaments which crown the bookshelves in the gallery. At one end is a half-length statue of the pope in an oval wreath of laurel, below which were to stand two spheres, one terrestrial and one armillary, symbols of the sciences to which the library was largely devoted.

Perhaps the most revealing fact about the library is that, when it was restored a few years ago, it was found that on the wall Borromini had drawn out in full scale and with his own hand – the style and the form of shading used are so personal that one can be in no doubt about this – the outlines and mouldings of the bookshelves. Such attention to detail was very rare among Roman Baroque architects, who usually relied on competent pupils to perform functions of this kind. It is more reminiscent of the scruples of a Poussin than of the methods of, say, a Pietro da Cortona, and it confirms what the writer of the history of S. Carlino says about the care and skill with which Borromini directed the execution of every detail in his buildings.

It is something of an anti-climax to go from S. Ivo to S. Maria dei Sette Dolori, and yet, small and unfinished though it is, this church has certain features of great originality which are not to be found in Borromini's other works. The convent, which belongs to the Augustinian Oblates, was founded by Camilla Virginia Savelli, who was married to Pier Francesco Farnese, Duke of Latera. In 1641 she acquired the land on which the convent is built and the church was begun in the next year. Borromini was chosen as architect and he agreed to undertake the job but said that he was too busy – presumably on the Oratory and S. Ivo – to do all the measuring. For this purpose he took on Antonio del Grande, who later built the gallery in the Palazzo Colonna and the wing of the Palazzo Doria facing the Collegio Romano, both works of originality and distinction.

91. Borromini: S. Maria dei Sette Dolori, Rome, interior

The structure of the church was complete by 1646 and the decoration of the interior was begun in 1648, though it was only finished in 1667 by Contini, who was also responsible for finishing the High Altar of S. Ivo. The interior [91] was disastrously restored in the nineteenth century, when Borromini's white walls were painted in bright colours, the columns with sham marbling and the vault with illusionist coffering.

In plan the church is a variant of the Oratory of the Filippini, that is to say, a rectangle with the corners cut off by curves, but in this case there is a shallow chapel protruding in the middle of each of the long sides. It is preceded by a vestibule similar in shape to the chapel in the crypt of S. Carlino. The church is articulated with columns set in niches, as at S. Carlino, of which the two flanking the entrance door are continued upwards by scrolls which merge into the architrave of the main entablature as the latter rises over the entrance in the form of an arch. In the middle an opening forces the scroll-architrave upwards so that it cuts across the frieze and impinges on the cornice, which at this point almost touches the bottom of the vault – a strange device which the architect did not use elsewhere.

The most remarkable feature of the church is the exterior [92]. The relation of the façade to the interior is like that at the Oratory. The door in the centre of the concave bay leads into the vestibule,

92. Borromini: S. Maria dei Sette Dolori, Rome, exterior

and the axis of the church runs parallel with the façade and not away from it, as one is led to expect. One of the side-chapels is enclosed in the curved projecting bay on the left, and this is balanced by a similar bay to the right containing the staircase. In its unfinished state the façade is tantalizing. The concave bay with the two sharply edged piers that flank it, though illogical in relation to the interior of the building, creates a form which is spatially exciting and no doubt would have been much more so if Borromini had finished it. As it is, we are left guessing how he would have linked the two halves of the design and what crowning feature he would have invented to bring the central section into relation with the projecting bays to right and left. Unfortunately the one known drawing for the façade only shows it up to the top of the pilasters and therefore does not help us to visualize what Borromini planned for the upper zone, but it shows that he intended the projecting elements to be flanked by another bay on each side containing a pair of niches one above the other, as in the existing part. There is actually a trace of one such niche in the right-hand bay, which suggests that Borromini began to carry out this section according to the drawing. The arrangement shown in the drawing would have excluded the present door on the right, which may also be an insertion by the architect – probably Antonio del Grande – who continued the building. The brickwork of the façade is rough and quite unlike the smooth surface of the Oratory, and it is almost certain that Borromini intended to cover it with stucco. Indeed the mouldings round the right-hand door, which are composed of thin tiles set on edge, are only comprehensible as supports intended to carry a covering of stucco.

In the drawing the central bay has a perfectly plain door, and this shows that the existing door is not from Borromini's original design. On the other hand the left-hand door shown in the drawing, which would have led into the middle of the church, is of an elaborate form not altogether unlike the existing door for the vestibule, so it is possible that the architect responsible for the two existing doors may have had sketches by Borromini to guide him. The same problem arises over the cloister. A drawing in the Albertina (XI) proves that Borromini made designs for the cloister, but it shows a much simpler scheme than the one executed. Each bay was to contain an upright oval window, flanked by two scrolls, whereas in the actual design the ovals of the windows are horizontal and they are enclosed in rather elaborate decoration composed of what might be Borrominesque motifs elaborated by a follower.

*

S. Ivo marks the climax of Borromini's career as an architect. Although he later had opportunities to work on bigger and more important commissions, such as St John Lateran and S. Agnese a Piazza Navona, there were always frustrating circumstances which prevented him from giving complete expression to his ideas. At S. Ivo he was free of such hindrances and able to display to the full his genius for spatial invention controlled by mathematical precision. S. Ivo was a startlingly novel work, but Borromini never lets his originality turn into caprice. The geometrical basis can always be felt through the fantasy of the form, and he breaks the rules of classical architecture as can only be done by one who knows them well. He is inventive but never whimsical; and he is eminently practical – a combination of qualities essential in a great architect.

# S. Giovanni in Laterano
# and S. Agnese in Piazza Navona

When Cardinal Giovanni Battista Pamphili was elected pope in 1644 under the name of Innocent X, Borromini's prospects suddenly seemed to become brighter. His friend and protector, Virgilio Spada, was summoned to the post of Almoner to the Pope and very soon became his adviser on all matters connected with the arts. Innocent took a liking to Borromini and preferred him to Bernini, who fell under the disfavour which struck all those who had been protected by the Barberini. Further, Bernini was at that moment particularly exposed to attack, because he was in trouble about the south tower of St Peter's, which he had begun to build without sufficiently strengthening the foundations, with the result that serious cracks had become visible in the lower part of the portico. Borromini behaved in an ungenerous manner over this affair and entered actively into the attacks launched on his rival, even making a beautifully precise drawing of the damage in the masonry. He then himself produced designs for towers which would be lighter and more suitable to their position. These were not carried out, however, and the whole project was abandoned till the early years of the nineteenth century, when the existing aedicules were put up by Giuseppe Valadier.

Borromini was also to be disappointed over the next commission which he received from the pope. Even before he was elected, Innocent had begun to rebuild the family palace on the Piazza Navona adjoining the church of S. Agnese, which he also took under his protection, and in 1647 he decided on a further step designed to make the Piazza practically a part of the Pamphili possessions. He commissioned Borromini to make a conduit to bring some of the water of the Acqua Vergine to the Piazza so that a fountain could be built opposite the church. This was to be constructed round an Egyptian obelisk which was lying broken in the Circus of Maxentius near the Appian Way. Borromini prepared designs, of which the only one known shows the obelisk supported on a simple base decorated on each face with a shell from which the water was to pour. At the suggestion of Prince Niccolò Ludovisi, Bernini also produced a design and, as he was out of favour, it was arranged that it should be smuggled into a room where the pope would see it. The effect was instantaneous and Bernini received the commission. The Fountain of the Four Rivers which he constructed in the square is in fact one of the greatest achievements of Baroque sculpture, and even Borromini's supporters must have realized that he could not have invented anything so brilliantly suited to the site or so well designed to satisfy the wishes of the pope.

This defeat was the first sign of Bernini's return to favour, but the pope did not lose interest in Borromini and in the next few years he received from him what were, from the public point of view, the most important commissions of his whole career.

Of these the most difficult was the restoration of the church of St John Lateran [93]. It had been a scandal for many years that this, the first church of Rome and one of the most venerated shrines of Christendom, had been allowed to fall into such a state of decay that it was in danger of collapsing. The walls of the nave were two feet out of the true at the top, and the columns of the nave arcade were too weak to carry the walls above them and had been encased in brick to make them stronger, thus destroying the character of the medieval basilica with its long row of re-used ancient columns.

In April 1646 Innocent decided to restore the church with the intention that it should be ready and opened for worship by the Holy Year of 1650. He appointed Spada to supervise the operation and Borromini as architect, and it is a tribute to their powers of organization – and to Spada's skill in handling an impatient patron and a difficult architect – that this prodigious undertaking was finished on time. Work began immediately, in fact so soon that it seems likely that Borromini had been preparing plans before the formal decision to restore the church had been taken; by the end of 1647 the structure was complete; by October 1648 the roof was finished; and in October 1649, two months before the opening of the Holy Year, the stucco decoration of the interior was completed.

The work was complicated by the fact that the pope insisted that as much of the old basilica as possible should be preserved. In this matter his approach was different from that of Julius II over the rebuilding of St Peter's, though even in that case it was regarded as desirable to include the area covered by the Constantinian basilica in the new church as far as was possible. Innocent's desire to pre-

93. Borromini: S. Giovanni in Laterano, Rome, interior, 1646–50

serve the old basilica was a reflection of the revival of interest in the early church and in Early Christian art which occurred in Rome in the first half of the seventeenth century. The catacombs were explored and the monuments found there were described and engraved in the two large folio volumes of the *Roma Sotterranea* published by Antonio Bosio in 1632; Cardinal Francesco Barberini restored the Constantinian Baptistery of the Lateran and sponsored the publication of Niccolò Alemanni's work on the mosaics of the Triclinium of Leo III at the Lateran in 1625; and Cassiano dal Pozzo had caused drawings to be made of the most important Early Christian and medieval frescoes and mosaics in Rome. The motives behind this activity were a mixture of piety and archaeological interest – more piety in the case of the pope, more archaeological interest in the case of Pozzo.

In the Lateran Basilica Borromini found that the outer aisles were so low and inconveniently arranged that he was compelled to pull them down and rebuild them completely, but in the case of the nave he succeeded in devising a scheme by which most of the columns were incorporated in the new structure and the upper walls were restored and strengthened. This meant that he did not have to take down the massive wooden ceiling put up by Pius IV, though it is known that he would have liked to replace it with vaulting. In fact the final decision to keep the wooden ceiling was not taken till the restoration had reached the level of the capitals of the main order.

At least one other architect submitted a design, which has survived [94]. The drawings are signed della Greca, and it is usually said that the author was Felice della Greca who built the steps in front of the church of SS. Domenico e Sisto, but he was only just over twenty when the Lateran project was first mooted and it is far more likely that Borromini's competitor was his father, Vincenzo, who had been papal architect under Urban VIII from 1631 to 1644 and might still have had hopes of gaining the favour of his

94. Vincenzo della Greca: Design for S. Giovanni in Laterano, Rome, drawing

successor. The mediocrity of this design serves to show up the brilliance of Borromini's solution. Della Greca proposed to have an arcade consisting of a single unit repeated seven times, with coupled pilasters standing on bases almost as high as the arches between

them. Borromini approached the problem in a quite different manner. His basic ideas were two: first to avoid the monotony of a bay
repeated seven times, and second to use giant pilasters rising straight
from the ground, thereby avoiding the awkward relation between
bases and arches which is so marked in della Greca's design. In the
use of giant pilasters he was following the example of Bramante at
St Peter's, but the idea of planning the whole arcade as a centralized
unit was a considerable break with tradition.

Borromini tried out a number of variants of these ideas, three
of which are recorded in surviving drawings [95, 96, 97]. These have
usually been treated as if they were successive projects, showing
the evolution of Borromini's ideas, but they are more likely to be
three alternatives presented simultaneously to the pope. This is confirmed by the account given by Martinelli when he says that several
drawings were shown to the pope, who settled on one of them, and
also by the character of the drawings themselves, which are identical
in size and technique and look as though they were all produced
simultaneously. Moreover the time available was so short that it
would hardly have been possible for the architect to have presented
a plan, then to have taken it away and modified it, and then repeated
the process a third time. In one scheme [95] the end bays of the
wall, which were solid in the old basilica, are treated differently from
the others and are left without openings. Along the remainder of
the nave Borromini pulled down one out of three of the old columns

95. Borromini: Design for S. Giovanni in Laterano, Rome, drawing

and built the other two into a solid pier against which he set his
giant pilasters. Between the piers he placed alternately tall round-
headed arches and low flat-headed openings with coupled columns.
There is also a subtle play on the shapes of the pediments in this

design The windows at the upper stage have alternately straight and curved pediments, whereas the small openings in the arcade have pointed pediments. These come below windows with curved pediments, so that there is a regular pattern with curved pediments in the windows coming above straight ones on the small openings below; but in order to carry this alternation right through, Borromini has used curved pediments for the niches in the end bays where they come below straight pediments over the windows. The second design [96] is only different from the first, in that the end bays have been opened up and the smaller bays of the main arcade have lost their pediments and have been made slightly wider by being carried

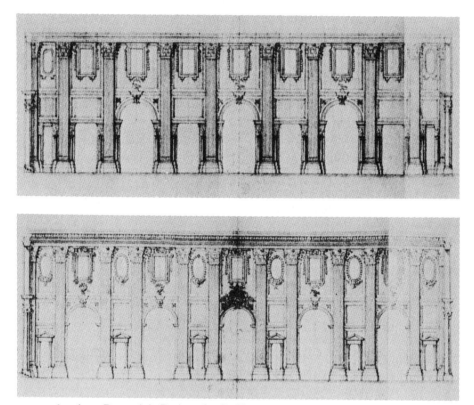

96 and 97. Borromini: Designs for S. Giovanni in Laterano, Rome, drawings

on single columns. In the third scheme [97], which corresponds basically with what was actually built and is presumably the one chosen by the pope, Borromini used an arrangement which altered the whole character of the design. He abandoned the idea of having three larger arches in the centre of the arcade and in effect went back

to a repeated bay, but to a bay so wide that it only needed to be
repeated five times instead of seven and at the same time produced
an alternating rhythm of large and small units right down the nave,
including the two end bays which had hitherto been treated as separate units. In this scheme he blocked the smaller openings and set
in them niches for statues, so that instead of an alternation of wide
and narrow openings he now has one of openings and solid piers.
The central bay is emphasized by a large trophy with the arms of
the pope.

Borromini's reasons for making this change are not recorded, but
he probably realized that, though in an elevation drawing the design
with alternating large and small arches is very effective, seen, as it
would have been, in fairly steep foreshortening, it might have looked
incoherent, because the spectator could not have grasped the basic
symmetry of the design from the entrance to the church or indeed
till he had got a considerable distance up the nave. In fact he could
never have stood far enough away to get the impression produced
in the drawing. On the other hand, in the true elevation shown in
the drawing for the last scheme it is impossible to appreciate one
of its most important features, the fact that the niches in the piers
project from the plane of the wall and by their movement bring
an element of variety into the whole design which prevents any
possibility of monotony. This effect of variety is heightened by the
fact that the niches are enclosed in verd-antique columns – taken
actually from the side aisles of the old basilica – and that their bases
and pediments are of dark grey marble, so that they stand out in
strong contrast to the white of the piers and pilasters.

The changes introduced between the final drawing and the actual
building are relatively small but not insignificant. In the building
the windows are alternately oval and rectangular, as in the drawing,
but the pediments over the rectangular ones are now of the Palazzo
Barberini type, except for those in the middle bays which have the
form used in the Capitoline palaces, which Borromini had used in
the first cloister of the Oratory. This change served two purposes:
it emphasized the middle bay of the nave and allowed the architect
to replace the heavy coat-of-arms which he had originally planned
by a much lighter shield, and it linked up the central bays of the
nave with the entrance wall of the church, where the same window
occurs in a shallow curved bay.

Two of the alterations are more crucial, because they imply a
fundamental change of plan for the vaulting of the church. Unfortunately the surviving drawings do not show how Borromini

originally intended to vault the building, but they imply either the preservation of the existing flat wooden ceiling or the introduction of a barrel or coved vault. In the actual building, however, he turns the bays of the nave nearest to the entrance [98] so that they cut across the corners at 45°, and along the nave he makes the entablature break forward, though only very slightly, over each pair of coupled pilasters. These two changes can only mean that he was planning the kind of ribbed vaulting which he had already used in the Oratory of the Filippini and was to use even more effectively in the chapel of the Collegio di Propaganda Fide. It is safe to guess that a pair of ribs would have sprung from the canted pilasters on either side of the entrance and would have ended on the second pair of pilasters on the other side of the nave, but it is difficult to be more precise than this, and the only reconstruction that has been proposed is not satisfactory. The most difficult problem is how the architect would have ended the vaulting at the crossing, because he did not cant the pilasters of the two bays of the nave before the crossing, and the last pair of pilasters stand behind two of the colossal ancient granite columns carrying the crossing arches, which Borromini presumably intended to preserve when he came to redecorate the choir and transepts as he hoped to do. The explanation may be that this last bay was built after it had become clear that the pope intended to preserve the wooden ceiling, so that the whole scheme for vaulting would have to be abandoned.

In the construction of the aisles [99, 100] Borromini was not hindered by having to incorporate earlier masonry, but he was obliged to follow the alternation of larger and smaller bays established by the design of the nave arcade. In fact he emphasized the inequality of the bays by making the small ones dark, while the larger ones are strongly lit by the windows which he was able to insert in the walls between the aisles, because, though the height of the inner aisles was imposed by that of the nave arches, he could make the outer aisles much lower and give them flat ceilings. This arrangement of stepped aisles, which, incidentally, followed the pattern of the Early Christian basilica, would have had the advantage of providing buttressing for the vault over the nave, if one had been built.

In spite of the hurry in which it must have been executed, the decoration of S. Giovanni in Laterano is of great beauty and very carefully thought out.

The bases of the giant pilasters [101, 102], which are in light grey marble, have the boldness which Borromini learnt from Michelan-

99. Borromini: S. Giovanni in Laterano, Rome, inner aisle

gelo combined with a Baroque fluency. On the pilasters themselves
the architect varied the width of the fluting as at S. Ivo, but less
emphatically, so that the effect is gentler. The design of the niches
is equally original. The dark grey marble bases are firmly curved
and project nearly – but not quite – at right angles to the plane of
the wall, and the mouldings round the panels at the back of the
niches – which are almost concealed by the statues – are as rich
as those on the door jambs in the Oratory. The palms [103] and
laurels surrounding the names of the Apostles are carved with the

100. Borromini: S. Giovanni in Laterano, Rome, outer aisle

101 and 102. Borromini: S. Giovanni in Laterano, Rome,
bases of pilasters in nave (*left*) and aisle (*right*)

103. Borromini: S. Giovanni in Laterano, Rome, base of statue of St John

same nervous crispness as those over the doors at S. Ivo. The rails [104] which separate the chapels rebuilt by Borromini from the outer aisles are of his usual type, but with a complication, because here they are set alternately with their pointed edges and their flat sides forward, whereas in the other examples the pointed edge

104. Borromini: S. Giovanni in Laterano, Rome, rail of chapel

always faces forward. This small change intensifies the effect of movement along the balustrade.

The symbolism of the decoration is as explicitly Solomonic as at S. Carlino and S. Ivo. Winged cherubs' heads abound [105], particularly in the aisles where they support the flat entablature of the lower openings and cling like bats to the vaults of the inner aisles.

105. Borromini: S. Giovanni in Laterano, Rome, detail of outer aisle

Pomegranates replace the eggs in the egg-and-dart mouldings on the capitals of the nave pilasters; and, although in most of the arches of the nave the sides and soffits are decorated with bands of laurel [106], on the two middle arches and in that over the door these are replaced by palms [107]. All the three elements taken from the Holy

106 and 107. Borromini: S. Giovanni in Laterano, Rome,
laurel-leaves and palm-leaves on pilasters of arches

of Holies are therefore present. A further biblical reference is to be found in the names of the twelve Apostles written below their statues. This probably refers to the descriptions of the New Jerusalem in Revelation (21:14), which had twelve foundations – *fundamenta* in the Vulgate – on which were written the names of the twelve Apostles of the Lamb, the word *fundamenta* being interpreted as bases.

The Lateran basilica was ready for use at the beginning of the Holy Year of 1650, but much remained to be done. Borromini's hope that the church would be vaulted was never fulfilled, mainly no doubt because of shortage of funds but perhaps also owing to the reluctance on the part of the pope to destroy the magnificent sixteenth-century wooden ceiling. Innocent intended, however, to carry on the work of restoration into the apse of the church, leaving out the transepts, which had been strengthened and redecorated in the early years of the century by Clement VIII, but the project was not carried out. Later, under Alexander VII, Borromini prepared designs for a new ciborium which was to stand at the crossing and to replace the medieval structure; but here again nothing was done.

In fact the only work done after 1650 concerned the nave. The mosaic floor was restored and relaid, and at almost the same time Borromini began work on the tombs in the side aisles. While the old basilica was being rebuilt a large number of tombs were of necessity removed. Some were destroyed, but in most cases fragments of them were moved to the cloister and stored temporarily. A short time before his death Innocent gave orders that some of the fragments of tombs belonging to the most important personages should be moved back into the church and incorporated in the new building. This work was only just begun when he died and most of the tombs were set up by Alexander, whose arms or symbols appear on all but a few of them. Innocent and Alexander were faced with the same problem which confronted Julius II when he began the rebuilding of St Peter's, but in the latter case an obvious solution was offered by the fact that St Peter's had an extensive crypt to which the tombs could be removed, whereas at the Lateran there was no crypt at all. Reinstated as they stood in a Baroque building the tombs would have looked incongruous, and Borromini arrived at the strange solution of taking fragments of the old tombs and incorporating them into new structures of his own design. The result to a medievalist is horrifying, but if the monuments are considered as re-creations of Borromini they are of great interest and, in their singular way, of great beauty.

108. Borromini: S. Giovanni in Laterano, Rome,
tomb of Cardinal de Chaves, after 1655

The monuments of the popes – Sergius IV, Alexander III and
Boniface VIII – were all installed against piers, where they had
ample space, but those of the cardinals were put against the walls
of the outer aisles, in which there were oval windows which had
to be taken into account and which greatly complicated Borromini's

109. Borromini: S. Giovanni in Laterano, Rome, tomb of Cardinal Giussano, after 1655

problems. As would be expected, he faced the problem directly and incorporated the windows into his designs.

The degree to which the remains of the earlier monuments were preserved in the new monuments varies very considerably. In some the whole sarcophagus with the recumbent figure is included and

Borromini has merely added a sort of frame to them [108]; in others either the figure or the sarcophagus survived; and yet others are reconstructed round figures of saints which do not always come from the tomb of the person commemorated. The strangest of all is that of Cardinal Giussano [109], in which the inscribed tablet alone belongs to his tomb and the panels with Gothic tracery come from the altar in the chapel of St Mary Magdalene, under which stood the tomb of Cardinal Bianco. The four monuments to the popes are almost completely the work of Borromini. That of Boniface VIII [110] incorporates a fragment of the fourteenth-century fresco celebrating the pope which decorated part of the nave wall

110. Borromini: S. Giovanni in Laterano, Rome, tomb of Pope Boniface VIII, after 1655

in the old basilica, and that of Sergius IV [111] has a half-length bas-relief of the pope blessing. In that of Silvester II, which was destroyed in the nineteenth century but is known from an engraving, and that of Alexander III [112], there seem to be no traces of earlier work.

111. Borromini: S. Giovanni in Laterano, Rome,
tomb of Pope Sergius IV, after 1655

As a consequence these papal tombs are the most complete
expression of Borromini's style. That of Alexander III consists of
an oval cylinder, like the aedicule of the façade of S. Carlino, set
against a simple curved niche composed of four massive columns
of unorthodox type, which carry an entablature decorated with a
band of laurel. In that of Boniface VIII the fresco fragment – of
which only the blank top part is visible in illustration 110 – is of
necessity set in a flat frame, but this is enclosed in a niche of which
the most striking feature is the very elaborate frieze, which includes
as its principal decorative motif the acorn of the Chigi arms. The

112. Borromini: S. Giovanni in Laterano, Rome,
tomb of Pope Alexander III, after 1655

ALEXANDRO III PONT MAX

arms of the Gaetani family are displayed above on a shield which appears to be composed of parchment and is the *ne plus ultra* of the style of strapwork which was invented at Fontainebleau in the mid-sixteenth century and later spread all over Europe. In the monument of Sergius IV the bas-relief is swamped by the surrounding frame of eight-pointed stars – which occur in the arms over the monument as well as in those of Alexander III – piled on top of each other but arranged so that single stars and pairs appear alternately. Outside this are two column-herms composed of cherubs with their wings covering the greater part of the columns.

In all the other tombs Borromini starts from the oval of the window, which he brings into his design in two ways. Above the window he adds a pair of winged cherubs' heads which frame the window rather loosely, but he shows the utmost ingenuity in fitting the architecture of the monuments themselves into the space left below the windows. In some cases he avoids the use of columns and creates a setting which is essentially sculptural, with consoles canted out from the plane of the wall and supporting the Chigi *monti*; in others he uses pairs of columns to perform the same function. Occasionally he introduces figure sculpture of his own, as in the tomb of Cardinal Annibaldi, where a crowned and grinning figure of death hovers over the figure of the dead man, while a snake winds its way across the back of the tomb.

In the monument to Cardinal Giussano Borromini invents a different solution and, stimulated perhaps by the forms of the traceried Gothic panels which he incorporates in the monument, he constructs over them a cusped architrave of which the side elements rise up, so that the curves of all three sections play against the oval of the window. The architrave is carried by four hooded herms which support baskets of pomegranates. At first sight they look as though they had come from a sixteenth-century garden fountain, but the hoods probably indicate mourning, and the pomegranates are symbols of eternal life. In the monuments of Cardinal Acquaviva and Cardinal Martiñez he sets the tombs against an actual colonnade, in one case with six, in the other with eight columns.

The most curious feature of all these tombs is that Borromini makes a definite attempt to create effects of false perspective in them. The ovals of the windows force him to make the mouldings of the parapets behind the recumbent figures or the entablatures of the colonnades curve downwards in the middle, and he takes advantage of this fact to make them look as if they recede. The effect is not one of complete illusion, as in the Spada colonnade, because circumstances do not allow of it, and it is closer to the partial illusion created in the top windows of the loggia in the Palazzo Barberini or in the half-domes in the church and refectory of S. Carlino. Seen, however, as no doubt they were intended to be seen, across the full width of the double aisle, the effect is to give the architectural structures of the monuments much greater depth than they actually have, and certain details make it clear that this effect was deliberately sought by the designer. For instance in the Acquaviva monument Borromini not only makes the inner columns lower and thinner than the two outer ones but places them closer together, so that the effect of perspective is almost complete. In the tomb of Cardinal Giussano the effect is more bizarre, but the architect's intention was apparently to create the illusion of a sort of Gothic shrine surrounded by three very flat arches, of which the middle one is seen frontally and the two side ones in very steep perspective. Admittedly in this case the result is scarcely convincing, but that it was intended is made clear by the fact that he makes the inner pair of herms considerably smaller than the outer pair.

The attitude towards the Middle Ages implied in the project for constructing these tombs is basically the same as the feeling which made Innocent X anxious to preserve as much as possible of the old basilica. It had nothing to do with admiration for the building or the monuments as works of art, since in the case of the building nothing that survives is now visible, and in the tombs the remains of the old were swamped by the new. The feeling was one of pious veneration for the monuments of the early Church, and was very close to the respect for the burial places of the martyrs which had led to the exploration of the catacombs. In fact the fragments of the old tombs are placed in their new settings much more like relics in an altar than works of art in an architectural whole.

This was certainly the official point of view, but it is possible that Borromini himself had a greater feeling for the fragments for their artistic qualities. The fact that he took the trouble to save the three tracerized Gothic arches from the chapel of S. Mary Magdalene is an indication of this, as they had no relevance to the tomb in which he incorporated them; and further evidence of his interest in medieval art is provided by the fact that he made a careful drawing of the wall of the old nave, showing a Gothic window and a large section of the medieval frescoes. Further, in one design for a decorative panel made for the Lateran but not carried out (Albertina 320) he introduces a blind arcade of pointed arches, completely Gothic in character.

It has been suggested that Alexander VII may have been pursuing a conscious, almost political line of thought in his choice of popes and cardinals to whom monuments should be set up in the restored church, and it is certainly the case that some of those honoured would have been persons for whom he would have felt particular veneration. Alexander III was, like him, a Sienese and a strong supporter of the temporal power of the papacy against the Emperor, and Boniface VIII had struggled – like Alexander and with equally little success – against the power of the French kings. But the other persons chosen for reburial do not seem to conform to any political pattern, and it is known that the sites of many papal tombs in the old church had been lost through fires or vandalism. It is in fact recorded that a mass of bones believed to come from the tombs of popes or cardinals were buried in the tomb set up in the new church in honour of Sylvester II. It is unlikely that out of this unpromising material Alexander would have been able to make a coherent programme of sepulture.

Apart from the tombs in St John Lateran Borromini was concerned with designing two other funerary monuments. In the case of the first, that of Clemente Merlini (d. 1642), a legal official at the papal court, which stands in a dark chapel near the High Altar of S. Maria Maggiore, it is not clear how far he was responsible for the design, which has few features characteristic of his style, but his friend Martinelli, who ascribes it to him, gives to the materials out of which it is constructed an interpretation in keeping with Borromini's mode of thought. The red and white of the veined marble, he says, are symbolical, the red standing for the strength of Merlini in his administration of justice, and the white for the purity of his character.

The other monument was erected in 1650 in the Oratory of S Venanzio in the Lateran Baptistery to Cardinal Francesco Adriano Ceva [113], who the year before his death had commissioned Borromini to build a new church and lodgings for the Noviciate of the Jesuits, though the plans were never carried out. It is much more typical of Borromini's manner than the Merlini tomb. It consists of a flat wall-tablet of black marble with a frame of peach-coloured marble decorated with roses in the same material and palmettes of great elegance in *pavonalezza*, a cream-coloured marble with slight purple markings. The coat-of-arms is in black and yellow marble, and the cardinal's hat and tassels are in *rosso antico*. The decorative features have the severity and tautness which are typical of Borromini in his maturity. In a note on a preliminary drawing for the

113. Borromini: S. Giovanni in Laterano, Rome, baptistery, tomb of Cardinal Ceva, 1650

114. S. Agnese in Piazza Navona, Rome, façade

monument Borromini tells us that he included roses because the cardinal died at an early age, and palms to symbolize the fame of his charitable works.

The story of the building of S. Agnese in Piazza Navona [114] is the saddest in the whole of Borromini's career. The church was the last and most important part of Innocent X's project for improving the Piazza Navona. The decision to pull down the old church of S. Agnese and to rebuild it on a much grander scale was taken in 1652, and the plans were supplied by Girolamo Rainaldi and his son Carlo. The foundations were begun immediately, but a year later, when the façade had reached the height of about ten feet and

the walls of the interior were finished almost up to the top of the
niches on the piers, the two Rainaldi were sacked, mainly on account
of criticisms which had been levelled at the design, and Borromini
was called in to finish the building.

Rainaldi's design consisted of a Greek cross with all the members
ending in apses [115]. In his first design he planned a straight façade

115. S. Agnese in Piazza Navona, Rome, interior

with coupled full columns, but it is possible that before he was dis-
missed he produced a new project with a slightly concave front. In
any case Borromini ordered the demolition of what had been built
of the façade. For the church itself he produced a plan in which
the piers were to be based on convex curves which continued into
the concavities of the arms, but he was forced to abandon this,
though in the actual building he modified the spatial effect by adding
whole columns to the edges of the four main piers, thus widening
them and making them more monumental. This change also
had the effect of altering the shape of the pendentives so that they
ended in broad bases instead of in points, as was usual in Roman
churches.

Borromini's design for the façade [116] was much bolder. It included an oval flight of steps, projecting well into the piazza, and
a reentrant central bay on eight full columns in two planes, over
which was a balustrade and a pediment, broken in form, which stood
out against the drum of the dome. The towers were of one storey

116. Borromini: Façade of S. Agnese in Piazza Navona, Rome, drawing

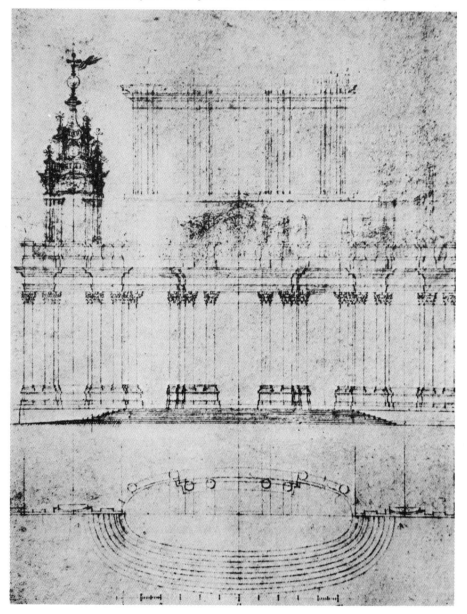

only, but they ended in superstructures composed of concave bays
with undulating balustrades between piers crowned with Pamphili
lilies. Work was carried out on this plan with such speed that by
the beginning of 1655 the facade was complete up to the cornice,
the dome was finished except for the lantern, and in the interior
the columns and pilasters of the main order were complete up to
their capitals. At this point however Innocent died and Camillo
Pamphili was left to complete the building. He showed little interest
in it and Borromini lost heart. There were complaints from the
workmen that he rarely visited the site and in due course Alexander
VII put Cardinal Imperiali in charge of a commission of enquiry.
In February 1657 the commission recommended that Borromini
should be got rid of and in order to avoid actual dismissal he
resigned. Carlo Rainaldi was called back to continue the building
and appears to have been responsible for most of the changes introduced into Borromini's design. He reduced the height of the lantern and gave it eight columns instead of the projected sixteen; at
the same time he added a storey to the towers but replaced Borromini's crowning feature with the mean structures that we see today.

Rainaldi is not, however, responsible for all the modifications to
which Borromini's design was subjected. In 1666 Camillo Pamphili
died and his widow Donna Olympia (Aldobrandini) took charge of
building operations. Within a few months she had appointed Bernini as a member of the commission with effective control of the
work. He introduced several important changes into the designs of
both the exterior and the interior. On the façade he replaced Borromini's bold pediment by the present one, which is straight and entirely enclosed in the attic. In the interior he designed the heavy
cornice and removed those parts of the attic over the main order
which ran under the pendentives, thus enlarging the field of the
latter, and he commissioned a young and almost unknown artist,
Giovanni Battista Gaulli, called Baciccio, to fresco this zone, quite
possibly supplying sketches – or at least suggestions – for the com-
positions.

In 1668 the young Camillo Pamphili came back from a long tour
abroad and took over the direction of the building from his mother.
He appointed Ciro Ferri to fresco the dome, and reinstated Carlo
Rainaldi as architect. The decoration of the interior was completed
by a group of sculptors who inserted high reliefs on a grand scale
and in coloured marbles over the three altars. This decoration of
frescoes and marbling is certainly not in accordance with Borromini's intentions. We do not know what he had in mind for the

church, but it would certainly have been something less rich in colours and materials, probably executed in white stucco and composed only of architectural forms.

The history of the building of S. Agnese accounts for its present unhappy state. As a background to the Fountain of the Four Rivers it is splendid enough, but as a work of architecture it is confused and full of conflicting elements. It is one of the most melancholy proofs of how seriously Borromini's difficult temperament could affect the execution of his designs.

# Domestic Architecture

Borromini's greatest achievements lie in the field of ecclesiastical architecture, but throughout his career he was involved in projects, which were often not carried out, for palaces and villas, generally for patrons with whom he was connected over the building of churches or religious houses.

The earliest of these projects – for the Palazzo Carpegna – proves that Borromini, given the opportunity, could have produced something of real originality in domestic architecture.

The story of the projects is complicated. At some date, probably in the early 1630s, the Conte Ambrogio Carpegna, a protégé of the Barberini, acquired the Palazzo Vaini – visible on the left of illustration 117 – at the north end of the block on the east side of the piazza in which stands the Fontana di Trevi. In 1638 he bought another house to the south of the palace from Pietro Schinardi, who owned the greater part of the block. By 1640 he had made further purchases of land and was in possession of the entire island enclosed on the north by the Piazza Cornaro, on the east by the Vicolo Scavolino, on the south by the Via del Lavatore and on the west by the piazza and the Via della Stamperia. Borromini's first plans (Albertina 1026, 1028, 1029) were made when Carpegna owned only the north end of the block and show a modest project which would have left the Palazzo Vaini untouched and extended it by a small wing along the Vicolo Scavolino and a narrow three-bay loggia facing the Via della Stamperia. Another drawing (1023) shows a variant of this scheme in which the loggia consists of two aisles, one of which continues the central corridor of the old palace. In another variant (1027) Borromini was to add an octagonal *salone* to the south of the old palace, and in yet another he replaced the staircase of the palace by an oval one, a feature which, with the loggia, was to survive and be incorporated in the building actually carried out, though in a different position.

The remaining drawings show a series of schemes for developing the whole site and must, therefore, have been made after 1640. In some of these (1009 f and g, 1031) the old palace is left intact, but the door in it facing the Piazza Cornaro is blocked and the only entrance to the palace would have been from the Via del Lavatore on the south, but other drawings present much more ambitious schemes, in which the awkward site – an irregular triangle with the apex cut off and a break in the east front – is given apparent symmetry.

The three schemes shown in this group of drawings have usually been treated as if they were successive stages in the evolution of an idea, but it seems more likely that they were alternative projects on which Borromini was at work simultaneously and which were probably presented to the patron at the same time. Two of the ground plans (1017a and 1019b) are almost twins in size and technique and show the parts of the existing buildings which were to be preserved in red in identical form, and the third (1015), though it does not have this particular feature, has so many details in common with one or other of the first schemes that it cannot be separated from them.

In one group of drawings the Palazzo Vaini is preserved intact and extended southwards in a variety of manners. In all of these a rectangular arcaded court forms the centre of the plan. In the simpler version [117] it is clumsily related both to the Palazzo Vaini and to the block at the south end of the island, since the passage which forms the spine of the former leads into one corner of the court and another passage, to the south entrance to the palace, leads

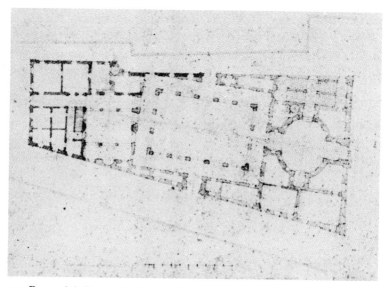

117. Borromini: Design for Palazzo Carpegna, Rome, drawing

off the middle of the opposite side. In this plan Borromini intended to alter the angle of the south front on the Via del Lavatore so that the passage would meet it more or less at right angles, but this would have involved losing some valuable land. In the second set of plans [118, 119] Borromini offered a more radical solution by changing the axis of the passage in the old palace so that it coincided with that of the rectangular court and the vestibule at the south end of

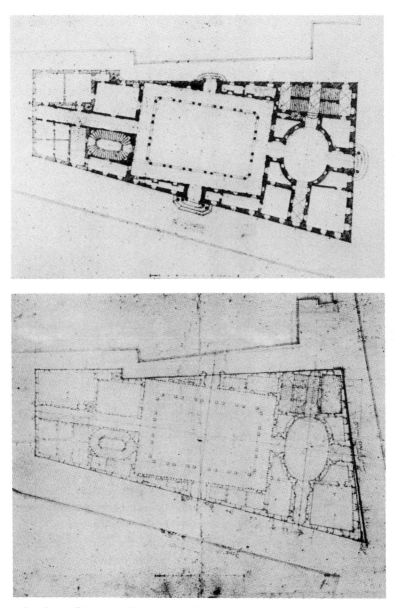

118 and 119. Borromini: Designs for Palazzo Carpegna, Rome, drawings

the site. In this scheme he intended to use a Serlian arch round the court instead of the regular repetition of a wide arch, shown in the first set of drawings discussed.

The door at the north end of the old palace was preserved in both these schemes, but it was evidently to be of quite minor importance – in fact a sort of back door – and the main approach was to be in the southern part of the area. The architect arranged two entrances, from the east and west fronts, which lead into the middle of the arcaded court, and he filled the south block with a large oval vestibule which the visitor would enter from the Via del Lavatore and from which he would have a view straight ahead right through the court and, to his right, a vista up the grand staircase, to which he gave two alternative forms, one on a square plan, and one a double staircase with the flights turning back on themselves. In the third scheme [120] Borromini replaced the rectangular court by an oval

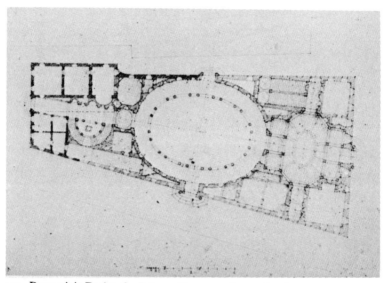

120. Borromini: Design for Palazzo Carpegna, Rome, drawing

one, also with Serlian arches, at the same time replacing the oval vestibule by an octagonal room connected with both the street and the court by triple loggias. This game of transferring a form from one feature to another seems to have been one of Borromini's processes of thought while he was working on the Palazzo Carpegna, because he used the elongated octagon which he now applies to the vestibule for the staircase in several of the other designs, and the oval was the basic form for the vestibule in the first scheme discussed

above [117]. In the last of these projects, however, the smaller staircase within the Palazzo Vaini has the very unusual form of a semi-
circle round an open well. As is shown in a detail drawing of the
staircase (1037), the visitor approaching this from the main court
arrived at the entrance to the staircase almost immediately and
reached the *piano nobile* at the end of a single semi-circular flight.

The variety of plans produced in these different projects bears
testimony to the extraordinary fertility of Borromini's imagination,
but in 1641 an event was to occur which was to stimulate him to
still further ingenuity. In November of that year, by a concession
of a kind very rarely granted, Carpegna was given permission to
add to his site part of a vacant plot publicly owned on the opposite
side of the Vicolo Scavolino, but it was made a condition that he
must leave the vicolo permanently free for coaches and foot pass-
engers. Borromini solved the problem of planning by using an oval

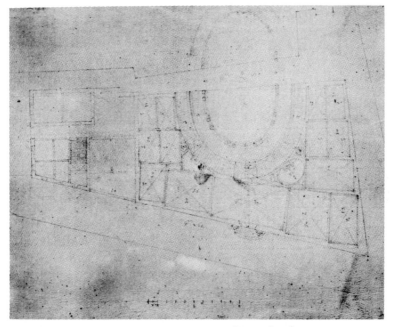

121. Borromini: Design for Palazzo Carpegna, Rome, drawing

court so arranged that its long axis ran across the street with one
half of the oval within the area occupied by the palace and the remainder on the other side of the vicolo [121]. The whole oval was
to be surrounded by a loggia supported on Serlian arches and, as
far as one can tell from the only surviving plan for this scheme,

the two parts of the loggia would have been joined by a bridge, which would have made it possible to get from one part of the palace to the other at the upper levels, though it is possible that in the area across the road the loggia would simply have carried a terrace. On the palace side of the road the loggia would have been surrounded by a staircase, though it is impossible to see from the plan how or where this would have been entered and to what point it led. One feature of this plan might seem to indicate that it must belong to an earlier stage than those just discussed. The Palazzo Vaini is preserved intact, as in the first group of designs for the whole site, but this is in fact logical because in this project the southern part of the palace round the oval court is completely cut off from the old palace, and there would have been no point in rebuilding it to change its axis.

Unhappily none of the projects evolved by Borromini for the whole site was carried out. In 1643 Ambrogio Carpegna died and the palace came into the possession of his brother, Cardinal Ulderico Carpegna, who immediately began to carry out a variant of one of Borromini's earliest and most modest projects. This scheme is shown on one sheet (1009b), drawn over one of the more elaborate plans with a rectangular court corresponding to No. 1015 (illustration 119). The Palazzo Vaini was left intact and was extended to the south by a loggia facing the Fontana di Trevi and leading to an oval ramp. The only element of fantasy remaining is the stucco decoration of the arch leading to the ramp [122], which is ingeniously broken at half its height to cover the section of the ramp which cuts across it at this point and is ornamented with cornucopias and other decorative features, probably symbolizing the hospitality which the owner of the house was supposed to offer to his guests.

The ramp itself is oval in plan, like Borromini's early staircase at the Palazzo Barberini, but it is set with its long axis across the line of the loggia leading to it, so that the visitor approaching it is unaware of its existence and sees only a niche with a statue in front of him till he turns right and sees the beginning of the ramp. The use of a ramp instead of steps is unusual in the seventeenth century but is a survival of earlier times when the owners of houses and castles liked to be able to ride up to the *piano nobile* on horseback.

The grand entrance planned by Borromini for the south end of the site, with its spacious vestibule and the vista up the staircase, would have been a complete novelty in the designing of Roman palaces, in which the entrance was normally narrow and the staircase separated from it, often by one wing of the loggia. Borromini's

122. Borromini: Palazzo Carpegna, Rome,
arch between loggia and staircase, after 1643

scheme would, however, have admirably solved the problem of access raised by the increased use of coaches in the mid-seventeenth century, which involved introducing wide entances to palaces and space to turn these cumbersome objects. Borromini's plan was not carried out and the first entrance of this type to be actually built was in the wing added by Antonio del Grande to the Palazzo Doria-Pamphili to make a monumental approach to the main apartments from the Piazza del Collegio Romano.

The plans for the Palazzo Carpegna are extraordinarily original and incorporate features which were quite unknown at the time. Roman palaces were invariably designed round square or rectangular courts and, though circular courts were to be found in other buildings, they were extremely rare. Raphael had used one for the Villa Madama and had been followed by Antonio da Sangallo the Younger in his plan for the Palazzo Farnese at Caprarola, and circular courts are to be found in some projects for very large palaces which never got beyond the drawing board, such as Serlio's plan for completing the Louvre and one of Inigo Jones's designs for Whitehall. No oval courts seem actually to have been built, though Serlio shows a very simple one, without arcade or colonnade, in the seventh book of his *Architecture*. Once again it seems probable that Borromini was inspired by an ancient example – or rather what he believed to be an ancient example – for one of the courts in Hadrian's Villa was shown in Pirro Ligorio's reconstruction as an oval surrounded by a colonnade composed of coupled columns, though modern excavations have shown that in reality it was a Greek cross with partly curved members. It was, further, a very bold idea to have planned to make the court run over the street to enclose the area owned by Carpegna on the other side. Such an arrangement has no parallel in earlier architecture, though there is some analogy with the way in which Pietro da Cortona was later (1656) to carry his façade of S. Maria della Pace over the streets which run along either side of the church.

Equally unusual are the forms which Borromini gave to the smaller elements of his design – semi-circles and elongated octagons for staircases, vestibules and smaller courts – and it required the greatest ingenuity on the part of the architect to fit these features into a coherent pattern and into a plan which would satisfy the practical needs of the patron. In the plan of the first floor reproduced in illustration 123 Borromini has also shown great skill in arranging

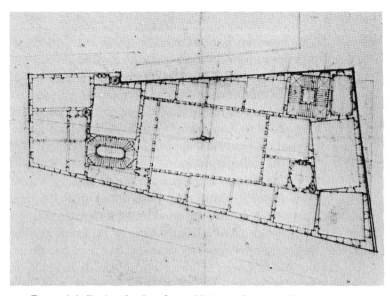

123. Borromini: Design for first floor of Palazzo Carpegna, Rome, drawing

the sequence of rooms in the irregular space available. Although
no room could have been of the same size or on the same axis as
its neighbour, he has concealed this fact as far as possible by arranging the doors in two enfilades running parallel to the outer walls
of the palace. Visitors arriving at the top of the grand staircase would
have seen in front of them two aligned doors leading into the two
principal reception rooms, from the second of which they would
have had a vista of five similarly placed doors, through which in
turn they would have passed to reach the vestibule of the octagonal
staircase, probably without noticing the changes in size and axis of
the rooms.

Next in order of date comes the remodelling and extension of the
Palazzo Falconieri. In 1638 Orazio Falconieri bought from Pietro
Farnese, Duke of Latera, a palace with a front of seven bays
running along the Via Giulia northwards from the church of S.
Maria della Morte, only a hundred yards from the Palazzo Farnese
itself. Behind this wing was a small court facing the river. In 1645
Falconieri acquired another house to the north of this palace, and
in the next year he commissioned Borromini to enlarge and remodel
the whole complex of buildings. Unfortunately the palace was much
altered when the Lungotevere was built in the late nineteenth century, but a considerable part of Borromini's work survives.

His hand is to be seen in three features of the palace: the street
front, the Belvedere and the decoration of some rooms in the north
wing of the palace. The street front is the least personal of the three,

124. Borromini:
Palazzo Falconieri,
Rome,
pilaster on street front,
after 1645

because Borromini was compelled to follow the pattern of the sixteenth-century façade which he extended from seven to eleven bays, adding a second door – now blocked up – to balance the first. The only personal features are the pilasters at the ends of the façade [124], which widen at the top in the fashion of Michelangelo's pilasters in the Medici Chapel and end in falcon heads, in allusion to the name of the owner of the palace. The façade has suffered from the thin stucco rustication which appears to have been added to the upper storeys in the nineteenth century.

On the top of the south wing he constructed a Belvedere facing the Tiber [125]. Seen from across the river this Belvedere instantly provokes comparison with Giacomo della Porta's loggia on the back façade of the Palazzo Farnese. Borromini was evidently conscious of the challenge and was determined to make the most of it. In certain ways he follows della Porta's model, but the variations which he introduces give his design a liveliness totally absent from the

125. Borromini: Palazzo Falconieri, Rome, front towards the Tiber

earlier architect's academic design. Della Porta's loggia consists of three arches, rather dry in their mouldings, separated by thin pilasters, and the whole is enclosed in the main mass of the palace façade under Michelangelo's monumental cornice. Borromini's loggia stands free above the rest of the palace, and indeed above all the neighbouring buildings, and it is crowned by a balustrade carrying Janus herms, which make a striking silhouette against the sky. Further, the loggia itself is much richer than della Porta's, because Borromini uses a Serlian arch – though with very narrow side openings – and the main piers have tall full columns standing in front of them. Finally he adds a personal note to the whole effect by giving the ends of the loggia a sharply concave form.

The rooms decorated by Borromini are very unusual for a Roman palace in two respects: they are small, and they are decorated entirely in stucco. In some cases the stucco was later painted in bright colours, and in two of the rooms the middle of the ceiling and the

126. Borromini: Palazzo Falconieri, Rome, ceiling

cove have been frescoed – probably in the late eighteenth or early nineteenth century – but originally no doubt the whole decoration was white, possibly touched with gold in some rooms.

The ceilings are among Borromini's most remarkable achievements in interior decoration. Some of them are based on elaborate curved patterns, one of which echoes the unexecuted designs for the fountain of the Oratory, but others are of almost Neo-classical sharpness, though they are always infused with the vitality which Borromini gives to even his lightest decorative schemes. One circular ceiling [126] is entirely decorated with vegetable forms: fleurs-de-lys, lilies, stylized sunflowers and the tense palmettes which Borromini had used over the central window of the Oratory. The stockade of the Falconieri arms and the lily of Florence, from which the family came, appear frequently, and on two ceilings the decoration incorporates explicitly symbolical features which are taken from two emblem books much read in the seventeenth century: Pierio Valeriano's *Hieroglyphica*, published in Basel in 1556, and the *Emblemata* of Junius Hadrianus, published in Antwerp in 1585. One of the ceilings has the sphere of the world surmounted by a snake eating its own tail (the symbol of eternity) round which hangs a laurel wreath, while through the circle formed by the snake runs a sceptre, on top of which is an eye. The first three objects signify eternal glory or fame, and the sceptre and eye stand for justice and vigilance, symbols appropriate to Orazio Falconieri, who was a prominent official in the administration of justice in the Vatican. In the next room the central motif of the ceiling consists of three interlocked laurel-wreaths which have not yet been traced to any precise model in the emblem books, though they are sufficiently close to one in Zincgreff's *Emblematum ethico–politicorum centuria*, published in Venice in 1648, to make it clear that there must be a common source in an earlier book.

In 1647 Borromini was commissioned by the Spanish Ambassador, the Conde d'Oñate, to remodel the palace on the Piazza di Spagna, which had just been bought from the Monaldeschi family for use as the Spanish Embassy, but, though his designs were so much appreciated by the Spanish king that he made him a Knight of the Order of St James of Compostela, only a small part of them seems to have been actually carried out. In the *Opus architectonicum* Borromini states that he had built the staircase in the palace on the same pattern as that in the Oratory, but unfortunately it was damaged by fire in 1738 and totally rebuilt in the nineteenth century. However, the vestibule which leads to it has several features which suggest that it was designed by Borromini. The vestibule is divided into three aisles by a colonnade of Tuscan columns linked by an abacus-architrave, an arrangement which repeats that used by Borromini in the cloister of S. Carlino, though here the columns are thinner and rather more meagre. The vault is supported by depressed arches like those in the corridor in the *piano nobile* of the Palazzo Farnese, ascribed to Michelangelo, a model which Borromini is likely to have studied, and the side aisles consist of asymmetrical openings like those at the end of the entrance vestibule of the same palace. Assuming that the original staircase occupied the position of the present one, the combination of vestibule and staircase would have made a small-scale version of the projected entrance to the Palazzo Carpegna, with the staircase leading off at right angles to the axis of the vestibule, so that the visitor getting out of his coach would find the first flight in front of him.

In the same year that Borromini designed the Palazzo di Spagna Innocent X called him in to advise on the building of the Palazzo Pamphili in the Piazza Navona, adjoining the church of S. Agnese, but although he produced ingenious plans, one of which included a reconstruction of the palace round a long court with apsed ends, the plans of the conservative Rainaldi were preferred and Borromini was only allowed a free hand in the construction of the *salone* [127]

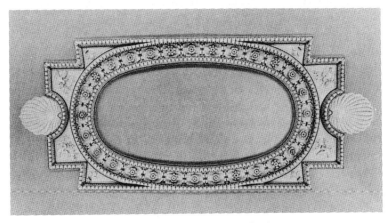

127. Borromini: Palazzo Pamphili, Rome, ceiling of *salone*

and the gallery running through the building next to the church [128], of which the great glory is the ceiling fresco by Pietro da Cortona. Borromini's contribution consists of the design for the end

128. Borromini: Palazzo Pamphili, Rome, gallery, after 1647

walls with windows in the form of Serlian arches and a series of doors on the long walls of the gallery. The scrolls ending in volutes over the tops of the doors are more characteristic of Cortona's style than of Borromini's, and it is possible that he incorporated into his design some features taken from drawings made by Cortona when he was painting the ceiling of the gallery. In fact one drawing in the Albertina (1125) connected with these doors may actually be a tracing from a design by Cortona. The hypothesis that Cortona made architectural designs for the palace is confirmed by the existence of a drawing at Chatsworth, apparently for a small circular chapel which has the Pamphili lily in the pediment over a panel intended to take a fresco and other smaller lilies in the frieze above.

Between 1650 and 1655 Borromini was at work on the Palazzo Giustiniani, opposite S. Luigi dei Francesi, which housed the great collection of paintings and ancient sculpture formed by the Marchese Vincenzo Giustiniani, who died in 1638. He made plans for a complete remodelling of the palace, but these were not carried out, and the only part executed was the main door to the palace, which, though it has a certain grandeur, lacks the liveliness usual in his work of this kind.

129. Borromini: Casino del Bufalo, Rome, door, engraving

Borromini also designed a door for the Casino which stood in the gardens of the Palazzo del Bufalo, near S. Andrea delle Fratte, and was destroyed in the nineteenth century when the Via del Tritone was made, but the design is known from a drawing (dated 1656) and an engraving of the early eighteenth century. The drawing shows an unexpectedly fussy design with Ionic capitals which include lions' heads below the volutes, but the engraving [129] shows a door in Borromini's most restrained style, with an oval window in the curved pediment and very severe swags of laurel looped round it. Both designs have the buffalo's head, the symbol of the family, in the top of the door.

Borromini's last datable palace was the Palazzo di Santo Spirito in the Piazza di Monte Giordano, commissioned in 1661 by Virgilio Spada, who was head of the hospital of Spirito Santo [77]. The palace, which was completely remodelled in the nineteenth century, is known from drawings by Borromini and from a late seventeenth-century engraving which shows how skilfully Borromini made use of the giant Doric order to make the palace, which was relatively small, stand up to the mass of the Oratory with its clock-tower which dominates the Piazza di Monte Giordano.

Borromini's work at the Palazzo Spada has usually been dated
to the years immediately after 1632, when Cardinal Bernardino
Spada bought the sixteenth-century Palazzo Capodiferro and began
to adapt it to his own use, but recently published documents show
that the most important addition associated with his name, the false-
perspective colonnade [35, 36], was built in 1652–3, a date perfectly
in accordance with the stylistic characteristics of the work, which is
composed of heavy Doric columns of the type used by Borromini
on the façade of the Collegio di Propaganda Fide and other late
works.

The documents also throw light on the question of how far Borromini was responsible for the design of the colonnade. The problem
is complicated by the fact that both the Cardinal and his brother
Virgilio, whose advice on architectural matters he constantly sought
but did not always follow, played a kind of game in which they got
plans or suggestions from one architect and then submitted them
for comments to another, or more often several others. In this particular case, however, it seems fairly certain that the original idea
came from Borromini, because the Cardinal wrote in a letter that
he wanted a colonnade of a type that he had seen in a temporary
*apparato* prepared by Borromini, probably for the Cappella Paolina
in the Vatican. On the other hand it must be noted that a similar
colonnade on a miniature scale had been made in 1647 for the tabernacle on the High Altar of S. Paolo Maggiore in Bologna, the choir
of which had been granted to the Spada family as a family chapel.
It is known that the general design of the altar itself had been
supplied about 1634 by Bernini, but the name of the designer of
the tabernacle is not mentioned in the documents. It would, however, be perfectly in accordance with the habits of the Spada family
to add a tabernacle designed by Borromini to an altar for which
the first idea had been given by his rival, though any design supplied
may well have been modified by Padre Giovanni Maria Bitonti who
actually executed the tabernacle and was, incidentally, also involved
in the Spada colonnade.

The colonnade, which has already been mentioned for its connection with a design by Montano, opens out of a small court to
the left of the main arcaded court from which it is separated by
the library. This has two big doors, one opening on to each court,
through which the visitor first sees the colonnade as he turns left
in the middle of the main court and approaches the library. The
view, which was till recently blocked by later alterations, has now
again been made visible, though the modern visitor – unless he is

especially privileged – is obstructed by glass doors and is compelled
to make a roundabout approach which to some extent destroys the
effect of the illusion.

The colonnade is an example of Borromini's ingenuity in making
use of limited space. The area between the court and the southern
boundary of the palace was very restricted, less than forty feet, but
he contrived to make the colonnade look far longer than this by making the two sides converge and reducing the height of the columns
as they recede. False perspective had been used in this way by Bramante in the choir of S. Maria presso S. Satiro in Milan, a church
which Borromini would certainly have seen in his youth, and by
Antonio da Sangallo the Younger in the entrance to the neighbouring Palazzo Farnese, but the illusion created by Borromini is on
an altogether different scale.

The effect of the colonnade has suffered from later alterations,
because it was intended that the vault should be interrupted at three
points to admit light from above, but two of these are now blocked
up, so that the effect of alternating light and dark has been destroyed
and the colonnade is now a continuously dark tunnel. The architecture of the colonnade is masculine and the Tuscan order simple
and massive. There are echoes of Michelangelo in the fluted consoles
on the façade facing the court which recall those in the Ricetto of
the Laurentian Library. Bernini was to remember Borromini's
colonnade when, in 1663, he came to design the Scala Regia as the
approach to the Vatican and the link between it and St Peter's. He
was to adapt Borromini's scheme to suit the different needs of the
case and he combined the effect of perspective with a lavish use
of sculpture on a heroic scale, but his debt to his rival's work is
unquestionable.

Borromini also received a number of commissions for the building
of villas. About some of these, such as the Villa Giustiniani and
the Villa Missori and one built for his friend, Fioravante Martinelli,
we have practically no information, but of two we know more,
though one has suffered many changes since Borromini's death and
the other was never built.

Much discussion has taken place about how far the Villa Falconieri at Frascati [130] can be regarded as following the design
of Borromini, and some critics have even maintained that it was
wholly built after his death and not according to his plans. It has now
been definitely proved, however, that the design was his and that
Specchi's engraving, made early in the eighteenth century, shows
it as he intended it to be. It was altered soon after this date by Fer-

dinando Fuga, who seriously damaged the effect of the facade by the insertion of extra windows. Fuga was also responsible for the gates in the wall surrounding the garden. In 1943 the villa was severely bombed in a raid on the German headquarters installed in it, but it has since been skilfully restored.

130. Borromini: Villa Falconieri, Frascati

The villa owes perhaps more to its superb position on the top of an olive-covered hill, with views over the whole southern Campagna, than to its actual architecture. The building was erected in the last years of Borromini's life – the only dated document is a bill for the completion of the work in 1667 – and it is likely that he was not able to give it the attention that he usually devoted to any job in hand. Further, he had to incorporate into his design an earlier villa built for Cardinal Alessandro Ruffini just before the middle of the sixteenth century. This consisted of a square building with towers at the four corners, two of which Borromini encased in the wings flanking the loggia on the principal façade. Borromini made use of the site, which slopes away from the façade, to establish the offices and stables in the two long side wings at a lower level than the central block, so that they were separated from the rooms lived in by the family but were still above ground. The effect of this is, however, much clearer in Specchi's engraving than in reality, because the visitor does not become aware of the difference in levels till he is quite close to the villa itself. The niche in the wall over

the loggia makes a fine centre to the whole composition, but unfortunately the decorative detail of this section is so poor as to
suggest that Borromini cannot even have supplied sketches for it.
The decoration of the interior was carried out after Borromini's
death, partly by Maratta and Ciro Ferri, who frescoed the ceilings
in five rooms, and partly by Francesco Grimaldi, who painted the
whole of one room with a continuous landscape – which is even
continued over the shutters – and so created one of the most spectacular effects of illusionism in Baroque painting in the seventeenth
century. Pier Leone Ghezzi painted the frescoes with portraits of
the Falconieri family on the walls of one of the rooms in which the
ceiling was painted by Ferri.

The villa commissioned from Borromini by Cardinal Camillo
Pamphili was never even begun, but his project is recorded in two
drawings [131] which were accompanied by a memorandum setting
forth the architect's ideas. The date of the drawings is not known,
but if, as seems likely, they were made for the villa which the Cardinal owned outside the Porta S. Pancrazio, they must have been made
soon after 1644, when he made the decision to build in the park.
In the event the architect chosen was Alessandro Algardi, who had
displaced Bernini as the official representative of the art of sculpture,
in which he was much more competent than in architecture. Since,
however, the villa was largely destined to hold the Cardinal's collection of antiques, it is arguable that his project was more suitable
than Borromini's, in which the sculpture would have had to take
second place.

The villa was to have been built like a fortified palace, with bas-
tions on the four corners, a form familiar in Italy since the fifteenth
century, when it still served a practical purpose, but which was often
used in later times – like the moat on many French châteaux – to
give a semblance of antiquity to a modern house. The plan shows
a central *salone* which probably ran through two storeys, octagonal
in form and strongly articulated with larger and smaller columns.
The shorter sides contained two small rooms each, and the longer
ones were filled with spacious loggias, each of five bays.

The whole building was to have been alive with sculpture, which
would certainly have competed dangerously with the Cardinal's
antiques. In the right-hand version the sculpture consists of figures
and busts disposed in oval niches on both floors, and in the left-
hand variant it would have included a free-standing equestrian
figure over one of the windows. In addition there would have been

full-length statues on the balustrade and round the dome, making a skyline unexpectedly broken for Borromini.

The fantasy visible in the whole conception of the villa would have been continued in the garden. Borromini proposed that the walks should be constructed between walls and so could be flooded while the Cardinal's guests were at dinner, so that afterwards they could go in small boats along the same avenues in which they had before walked on foot. Jokes such as this were common in the court life of Italy and other countries and go back at least as far as the fifteenth century, when Alphonso II of Naples was able at will to flood the sunken courtyard at Poggio Reale in which supper was served, but it was rare for them to be conceived on so large a scale. In addition there was to be a menagerie divided like Noah's ark into three tiers for the different types of animals, which were to be represented by live specimens if they were available, and by paintings or models if they were not. The reference to Noah's ark probably had a particular significance in relation to the patron, because the Pamphili emblem, the dove with the olive branch in its beak, was a direct allusion to the dove sent out of the ark by Noah which returned with the olive branch as proof that dry land was near.

But, as usual with Borromini, fantasy was combined with practical sense, for in the opening sentences of his letter presenting his project to the Cardinal he dilates on the fact that it would be foolish to compete in size or grandeur with the villas which already existed in Rome, and emphasizes the point that his plan would provide a villa small in scale but so rich in ingenuity that it would catch the attention of all visitors, and would cost no more than a simple building of the same size.

Borromini was involved in one further scheme for the Pamphili, but in this case the patron was Donna Olimpia Maidalchini, the pope's formidable sister-in-law. She had plans for improving the little town of S. Martino al Monte Cimino, a seat of the Maidalchini family. The most important part of the project, the reconstruction of the main street of the village on a systematic plan, was already in the hands of the architect Marcantonio de' Rossi, and Borromini seems only to have been called in to build the entrance gate to the town and to make improvements to the palace and the church, a medieval building which formerly belonged to a Cistercian monastery. His plans for the church were not carried out, and the spiral staircase which he built in the palace was destroyed in the eighteenth century, so that the only part of his projects to survive was the town gate, a severe and impressive structure of unusual form in that it

131. Borromini: Design for Villa Pamphili, after 1644, drawing

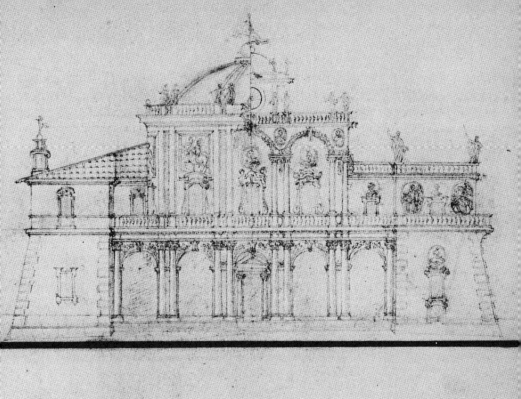

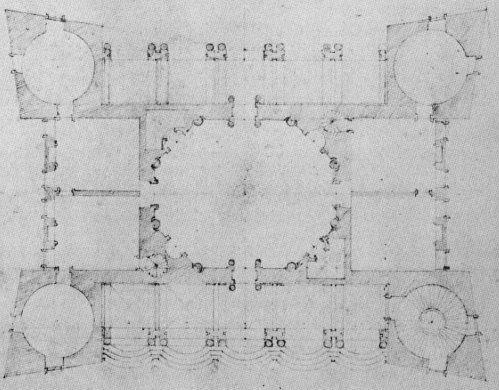

narrows towards the top. This form of door is to be found in Etruscan tombs, of which there are many in the district, but a more accessible source was an engraving in the fourth book of Serlio, in which such a door is shown. There is also a great similarity between the gate at S. Martino al Cimino and the entrance to the Castel S. Angelo, but this does not help to solve the problem, because, though it used to be believed that this gate dated from the mid-sixteenth century, it is now known that it was erected by Urban VIII and it has even been ascribed – though without conclusive evidence – to Borromini himself, though G. B. Mola, in his guide book of 1663, states that it is by Bernini.

# The Last Phase

The death of Innocent X in 1655 meant the end of Borromini's hopes of papal patronage, but he was far from inactive in the remaining twelve years of his life, though the new commissions which he obtained were rare and they were all of minor importance. Most of his time was spent on the completion of commissions which he had received earlier. We have seen how he lost the job of completing S. Agnese, but work on the tombs in the Lateran lasted for many years, and in the 1660s he was also concerned with the completion of S. Carlino. There was one further scheme of importance on which he was involved in his last years, the building of the Collegio di Propaganda Fide, with which he had officially been associated for some time, though little work had been done there during the pontificate of Innocent X.

The history of the institution goes back to 1622, when Gregory XV created a Congregation of Propaganda Fide as the organizing centre for missions which were beginning to play an increasingly important part in the policy of expansion of the Roman Catholic Church. Five years later, in 1627, Urban VIII founded the college, called after him the Collegium Urbanum, for the training of young missionaries. The Congregation was installed in a palace facing on to the Piazza di Spagna, known as the Palazzo Ferratini, which had been presented by a Spanish priest, Juan Bautista Vives. In 1634 Bernini had built to the south of the palace a chapel dedicated to the Three Kings and often referred to as Re Magi. In 1642 it was decided to rebuild the façade on the Piazza di Spagna and designs were prepared by a Theatine, Father Valerio, but they were modified by Bernini before they were actually carried out in 1644. Between 1639 and 1645 a wing with rooms for the seminarists had been begun by Gaspare de' Vecchi along the Via dei Due Macelli, which bounded the site on the north-east.

By 1646 the Congregation had acquired the whole of the island of which these buildings formed part and which extended to the Via Capo le Case to the south, where it faced the monastery of S. Andrea delle Fratte, and in that year Borromini was appointed architect to the College with the task of completing the buildings on this newly acquired land.

The problem was in many ways like that which had faced him at the Palazzo Carpegna: an irregular site with hardly a right angle in it, and an existing palace on one end of the area which had to be incorporated in the new scheme; but here there was in addition the need to integrate a church into the whole complex.

Borromini was first engaged on finishing the north-east wing and in making plans for the remainder of the site. These were accepted in 1647, but work was frequently interrupted owing to lack of funds, with the result that building dragged on till 1664, three years before the architect's death, and parts of the upper storeys were still being built after his death.

In the first scheme Borromini intended to incorporate Bernini's church into the new building, but he soon abandoned this project, presumably on the grounds that the church was too small, though one cannot help feeling that he would have felt a certain pleasure in pulling down one of his rival's buildings. His next plan [132]

132. Borromini: Plan for Collegio di Propaganda Fide, drawing

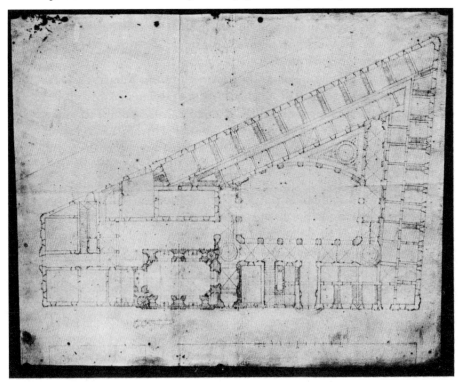

shows a larger church, covering the area occupied by Bernini's church and extending northwards to take in part of the site of the Palazzo Ferratini. The main entrance to the College was to be to the south of the church and led to the court in which Borromini planned to produce an effect of symmetry by constructing a curved arcade which would have continued the loggia on the other three sides of the court and concealed the fact that the court actually extended in a triangle towards the south-east corner, where the wings on Via Capo le Case and Via dei Due Macelli met. This arcade was never built, and that on the west side was later blocked up, so that the court now has completly lost its intended form.

Bernini's church was built on an oval plan with the short axis leading to the High Altar, as in his later church for the Noviciate of the Jesuits, S. Andrea al Quirinale. Borromini immediately changed this and his first design is for a very long oval church, with the principal axis running parallel to the façade, not at right angles to it as with Bernini's church. The oval, incidentally, was set out as the basis of tangential circles and equilateral triangles, on the system which the architect had used since S. Carlino. At this stage, although the main entrance to the church was from the corridor leading from the entrance, Borromini left a door straight on to the street on the cross-axis of the oval, but in his later schemes he abandoned this as being unnecessary in a chapel which was designed purely to serve the needs of the College. At the same time he changed the form of the church to a rectangle with rounded corners [133], and he planned to cover it with a vault of cross-ribs [135]. In both these features he was taking up themes which he had used at the Oratory, but he treated them with much greater skill.

At the Oratory the corners of the room are cut off by short straight facets from which spring single ribs, which, like all the others, abut on the central oval panel of the vault. In Re Magi the corners are rounded and flanked by pilasters [134, 135], so that pairs of ribs are projected across the vault. Further, their course is not interrupted, because the central decorative panel is now a hexagon formed by the ribs themselves. The arrangement is not, however, one of exact repetition, because, whereas one rib comes down above a pilaster on the opposite side of the church, its neighbour ends on the vault over the central window. In this way a pattern of extreme ingenuity is established, far more subtle than that which Borromini had used in the Oratory.

For the elevation of the side walls of the church Borromini hesitated between two projects which he shows side by side on a single

133–5. Borromini: Collegio di Propaganda Fide, Rome, chapel, after 1647
*Opposite above*, chapel
*Opposite*, detail of base of pilaster
*Above*, vault

136. Borromini: Drawing for chapel of Collegio di Propaganda Fide, Rome

drawing [136]. One shows a giant order of Corinthian pilasters running right up to the spring of the vault with its entablature covering the galleries. In the other the order is Ionic and the pilasters are shorter, so that the capitals come half way up the galleries which interrupt the entablature. The second arrangement is less tidy than the first, but Borromini chose it, presumably because it enabled him to insert large windows in the vault to allow more light to penetrate the church.

The new plan provided space under the galleries for four sidechapels which are surprisingly simple in shape, being rectangular with apsed ends, like those which Borromini had built at the Lateran. In fact the whole church is conceived in much simpler terms than either S. Carlino or S. Ivo, but it is none the less satisfying for that. The simplicity of the plan is carried on in the elevation and the decoration. The walls are divided by a straight entablature carried by the severe pilaster panels which flank the openings to the chapels; the lower windows are simple rectangles and the upper ones oval, but having simpler forms than those shown in either version of the drawing; and apart from the arms of Alexander VII over the High Altar the only decoration consists of the busts in niches on the piers, which stand on plain oval cylinders of black marble, echoing the form which Borromini had used for the tomb of Alexander III in the Lateran but without its curved superstructure. These bases and busts were only put up after Borromini's death and do not exactly correspond to the form shown in the only surviving drawings, but they are probably from his designs.

Of the decoration which Borromini planned for the rooms in the College very little was carried out, though there are fine doors on the *piano nobile* and ceilings of ingenious shapes in the vestibule of the library and the private chapel, now called the Cappella Newman, because Cardinal Newman celebrated his first mass there. Some idea of the decorative features which Borromini planned for the other rooms can be gained from a series of drawings [137, 138] for doors, windows and fireplaces in which the architect combines traditional and novel elements in an unusually brilliant manner. One

137 and 138. Borromini: (*left*), drawing for attic window on façade of Collegio di Propaganda Fide, Rome; (*right*), drawing for fireplace in Collegio di Propaganda Fide, Rome

is a variant on Vignola's fireplace in the Palazzo Farnese; another has the inverted, curved pediments invented by Buontalenti for the Porta delle Suppliche in the Uffizi and used by Bernini – or was it really Borromini who was then working in his studio? – in the door of the chapel of the Crucifixion in St Peter's. Two other designs are built up round the Chigi arms. In one the *monti* are supported on the middle of the mantelshelf over a winged cherub's head and enclosed in a structure made up of two scrolls, edged with palms, which curl outwards to support an oval frame, probably, one may surmise, intended to contain the bust of the pope.

Borromini showed equally great inventiveness in designing the façade of the College [139]. He hesitated about the exact form of the entrance, planning at first to have two doors, one next to the church and the other on the axis of the court separated by three bays of windows [132]. Then he brought the two doors together in a single bay, an awkward design which he soon abandoned. Finally he decided on a single door in the bay next to the church, which provides easy access both to the latter and to the court.

In all except the very earliest of his schemes, in which he planned a simple straight front, it is clear that Borromini had decided, as at the Oratory, not to be tied to making the façade correspond to the interior of the church, but here he is more successful in relating it to the College as a whole. Having fixed the door in the centre of the façade, he at first planned to have a façade of only five bays, but changed it to a seven-bay design, which had the advantage that the three left-hand bays covered the length of the church and the three on the right corresponded to the vestibule and staircase of the College. The resulting design, therefore, corresponded to the principal elements of the College, leaving two unarticulated wings at the ends, one of which merged with the Palazzo Ferratini and the other with the simpler architecture of the wings containing the cells for the seminarists.

The façade [139] is an extraordinary mixture of severity and fantasy. The design is based on giant pilasters of extreme simplicity but which conform to no known order. By a sort of inversion of the normal practice they are unfluted, except in their capitals, which have five grooves separated by very narrow slits up which run mouldings as fine as a knife-edge ending in arrow heads. The entablature is reduced to a cornice with modillions arranged in an irregular manner, so that they can be read in two ways: either as two modillions over each pilaster and two in the intervals, or as pairs of modillions close together, formed of one over the edge of a pilaster

139. Borromini: Collegio di Propaganda Fide, Rome, façade

and one over the interval. In the central bay the rhythm accelerates, so that there are two modillions over each pilaster, then two very close together, and finally a single modillion in the middle over the central door and window. In plan the façade is basically straight, but the central bay is set back in a concave bay, and the two end pilasters are set at an angle to the plane of the front facing, unexpectedly, away from the centre. This disposition is carefully calculated to take into account the fact that the College faces on a narrow street and the façade is always seen in steep foreshortening. It was probably for this reason that Borromini did not introduce a pediment over the middle section, because, given the site, it would never have been seen to any effect.

Above the cornice is a high attic with windows of fairly complicated design set in the plane of the wall. Those of the first floor are even more original and show Borromini's ability to think in terms of the plane and of depth, of treating the wall architecturally or carving it out of the block like Michelangelo. The windows in the side bays are concave in plan and are articulated with Doric columns and pilasters. The middle windows of these side sections have pairs of columns on a simple continuous curve, but their entablature is treated in a highly unorthodox way. It is split so that the top moulding of the cornice turns upwards and ends in scrolls which carry the pediment, which is not continuous but breaks forward in the middle over a cluster of four guttae, a sort of echo of the Doric order below. The space under the pediment is filled with a circular opening surrounded by palms. The side windows are simpler in elevation in that they are covered by round-headed arches, though it will be noticed that the arches are slightly stilted. Below this level the arrangement is unexpected. Instead of a pair of columns there is a pilaster and a column on each side of the window. The pilaster is placed flat against the wall, but turns round to form the edge of the niche in which the window is set, where it is equipped with another triglyph. The architrave and frieze disappear behind the column but reappear to form the central part of the niche. The columns are set at an angle to the plane of the wall and stand out from the niche as units completely separate from the pilasters, even having triglyphs on the sides of the impost blocks over the capitals. They are not, however, as completely independent of the pilasters as appears at first sight, because in the middle the order based on the pilasters has lost its cornice which turns upwards to follow the arched top of the window, and in the central bay the order has to 'borrow' the cornice of the columnar section, thus leading to an

ambiguity which one would expect to find in the late sixteenth century rather than in Borromini.

In the middle window [140] features from both types used in the
outer bays are combined, but with the basic difference that the
whole window is set against the concave wall of the central niche.
On each side of the window are two columns separated by a broken
pilaster. The outer column and the outer half of the broken pilaster
are set against the curve, but the break in the pilaster initiates a
convex curve which runs through the whole middle section and
encloses an oval space, the covering of which is decorated with the
dove of the Holy Ghost in stucco. The relation between the two

140. Borromini: Collegio di Propaganda Fide, Rome, central bay of façade

columns is complex, because they are each set orthogonally to the curve against which they stand, but this makes them just not at right angles to each other. Further, the sections of the entablature over the columns follow the curve of the niche and so add yet another complication to the whole effect.

At first sight the door seems simpler than the windows, but this is an illusion. The hood follows the familiar pattern of the Palazzo Barberini window, but in the three-dimensional version which the architect used at almost the same time in the door to the cloister of S. Carlino. The lower part is more complicated. The door is flanked by two piers which are neither columns nor pilasters. In plan they consist of two sides and two half-sides of a hexagon, each side being slightly concave, an effect that is even more reminiscent of late Gothic than the octagonal capitals in the cloister of S. Carlino. Further Borromini has taken up Michelangelo's innovation in the Ricetto of the Laurentian Library and has made his piers narrower at the bottom than at the top, and to this he has added his own trick of making the flutings of unequal size. Drawings for the door and the central window show that Borromini intended to make them considerably richer. The door was to have had in the pediment the arms of Urban VIII as founder of the College, and the pediment of the window was to have been flanked by the Chigi *monti*, which would have appeared again over the main cornice.

Martinelli expatiates with pride on one detail of the façade, namely the fact that Borromini uses Roman Doric columns without bases, a feature which is very rare in sixteenth- and seventeenth-century Italian architecture. The College, he says, was

built with beautiful architecture by Cavaliere Borromini, who, working as always according to the true principles of architecture and imitating the Ancients, may seem to those ignorant in this profession to have sometimes gone beyond the rules and to have worked according to caprice, outside these rules, as for instance in the façade of this church, in which he has used a Doric column which the Ancients made without a base, as is testified by Andrea Palladio in his book on architecture, Book I, chapter 15, and by other writers, and as we can see in the palace of the Savelli family, which was formerly the theatre of Marcellus, and which is recorded by Serlio in the second book of his *Architecture* and by Bernardo Gamucci in his second book on the antiquities of Rome, and was praised by Lomazzo in his treatise on painting, Book 6, chapter 45, p. 408. Buona Rota [i.e. Michelangelo] was esteemed so much because he worked as he wanted but with reason, by order and measure, as the said Lomazzo notes in the same chapter a passage which can be taken as a further declaration of Borromini's own faith in reason and measure and of his reliance on Michelangelo and the Ancients.

Borromini's one important new commission in his last years came from the Marchese Paolo del Bufalo, for whose Casino he had designed a door. In about 1653 Bufalo commissioned Borromini to complete the church of S. Andrea delle Fratte [141], which stood across the road from the Collegio di Propaganda Fide and near his own palace, and which had been begun in 1605 by an undist-inguished architect, probably Gaspare Guerra of Modena, who

141. Borromini: S. Andrea delle Fratte, Rome, dome and campanile, after 1653

built only the nave. Borromini was to build the choir, transepts and crossing, over which he was to construct a dome.

For the dome he followed the Lombard method which he had employed at S. Carlino and S. Ivo and encased the cupola in what appears to be a drum; but here it is a drum of even more remarkable design than that of S. Ivo. Its resemblance to the late Roman tomb near Capua, called the Conocchia, has already been mentioned, but it is even more important to notice the differences which distinguish it from its model. Of these the most significant is that, whereas the frontispiece in the middle of each bay in the Conocchia projects on a rectangular plan, in S. Andrea the section is curved, so that Borromini establishes a continuous double S-curve, like that on the façade of S. Carlino, on each face of the drum. A rough sketch in the Albertina (107) shows that at one stage he contemplated constructing an oval dome, but this seems to have been vetoed and he was compelled to follow a conventional circular pattern – perhaps left by Guerra – with the result that in the interior the crossing and choir are completely lacking in character.

Unfortunately the dome never received its lantern, but from a drawing [142] we can guess at its general form. This drawing, which is unusual in that it gives the plan of the building at two levels – the drum and the lantern – shows that the two elements would have been knit together very closely. The buttresses supporting the lantern would have sprung from a point immediately over the columns of the drum, but they would have been on curves which went much further back towards the centre of the structure and so would have enclosed a lantern of relatively small size. The form of the lantern is only roughly indicated in the drawing, but it would have had pairs of pilasters which fell exactly over the inner shell of the drum. It is difficult to visualize what it would have looked like, but it is clear from the plan that its concave bays would have made a contrast with the convexity of the drum in a manner wholly characteristic of Borromini.

The drawing is also interesting as evidence of Borromini's extraordinary consistency. It shows him in his last years still using the method of setting out his plans which he had employed in his youth. The construction of both the drum and the lantern is based on a series of concentric circles, the largest of which defines the convex bays. The axes of the four piers lie on diameters of the circles which bisect the angles between those of the four openings, and each pier and each opening occupies an angle of 45°. The oval curves of the reentrant bays are drawn on the usual system of tangential circles,

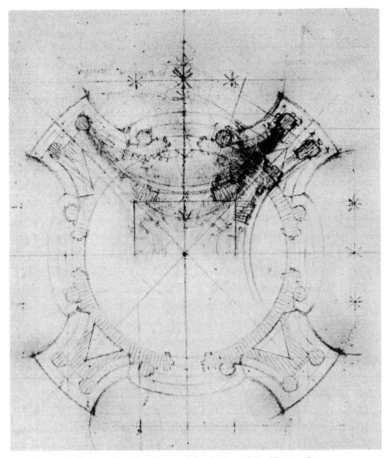

142. Borromini: Drawing for dome of S. Andrea delle Fratte, Rome

and the curve of the concave bay of the lantern is an arc of a circle with its centre at the point of contact of the two first circles. Borromini has marked the centres of these circles and their point of contact with stars as if to emphasize their importance. As it stands today, the dome is a mass of vigorously shaped rough brick-work which has for us the charm of looking like an ancient ruin in the Campagna, but there is no doubt that it was intended to be stuccoed. Compared with the façade of the Oratory the brick-work is very rough, and the capitals are made of thin bricks, almost like tiles, sticking out, which were clearly intended to hold the stucco facing, as in the church of S. Maria dei Sette Dolori.

The lower part of the campanile is also of brick, though the forms are somewhat simpler than those of the dome, but the upper sections are of painted stucco. The cylindrical section, which is based on an ancient model, as was pointed out in Chapter 2, is the most classical structure that Borromini ever produced and makes a striking and clearly intended contrast to the complex forms of the dome, and also to those of the superstructure above it. This consists of eight herms ending in winged cherubs, like those on the tomb of Sergius IV in the Lateran, separated by narrow curved recesses. Above them is a crowning feature composed of buttresses leading upwards and inwards to a narrow cylinder, an arrangement which would have echoed the form of the lantern on the dome; and the whole tower culminates in a flame-like form, incorporating the buffalo's head of the patron's family and the coronet of a marchese. As it stands today, the tower is taller than the dome but, if the lantern of the latter had been built, it would have stood out still higher and the tower would have taken its correct place as a support for rather than a competitor with the dome.

Something of the delicate severity visible in the columned cylinder of S. Andrea delle Fratte appears in the little chapel of S. Giovanni in Oleo [143], which stands by the Porta Latina, on the spot where the abortive attempt was made to boil St John the Evangelist in oil. The chapel was built in 1509 at the expense of a French ecclesiastic called Benoît Adam by an unknown architect probably from the circle of Antonio da Sangallo the Elder, though it was for long ascribed to Bramante. In 1658 Borromini was called upon by Cardinal Francesco Paolucci to restore it. He left the walls standing, redecorated the interior, which received frescoes by Lazzaro Baldi, a pupil of Pietro da Cortona, and added a new roof. The decoration of the interior is of no great interest, but the roof is an unusual construction. A drawing by Borromini shows that he at first intended to cover the church with a dome slightly higher than a hemisphere, the ribs of which were to be formed of palm branches, presumably in allusion to the saint's martyrdom. Then he tried a stepped dome, and finally decided on the present arrangement with a high attic and a low conical roof, a form which is certainly more appropriate than the other to the simple architecture of the sixteenth-century chapel, and which is taken from the ancient Roman models, such as the circular temple beside the Tiber, which in Borromini's day already had the roof which we see on it today, or the relief in the Uffizi which he had used for the campanile of S. Andrea delle Fratte. The attic is decorated with alternating palmettes and rosettes, the latter being, as Borromini tells us in a note on the drawing, the heraldic device of the patron. On the top of the roof is a strange

143. S. Giovanni in Oleo, Rome, 1658

structure, forming a sort of lantern and composed of the ends of the palm-leaves which were to have defined the ribs of the dome, and on this stands a sort of cube, each face of which is formed by a heraldic rosette. The mixture of austerity in the attic and fantasy in the 'lantern' is typical of Borromini's manner in his last years and is also to be found in another work which must date from about the same time, the frieze round the outside of the Lateran Baptistery, composed of trophies and the *monti* and oak-trees of the Chigi arms. The work has never been associated with the name of Borromini, but Martinelli states categorically that it was made for Alexander VII by him, and it is entirely in conformity with his late style.

An estimate of the other works connected with Borromini's last years is made more difficult by the fact that in each case there was interference by other architects, so that it is hard to distinguish Borromini's own share in the design.

144. S. Giovanni dei Fiorentini, Rome, High Altar

145 (*opposite*). Pietro da Cortona: Design for High Altar
of S. Giovanni dei Fiorentini, Rome, drawing, 1634

The first is the Falconieri Chapel which occupies the choir of
S. Giovanni dei Fiorentini [144]. This was planned by Borromini's
patron, Orazio Falconieri, as a family chapel where he and his
brother, Cardinal Lelio Falconieri, were to be buried, and in due
course room was to be found for younger generations of the family.
Work was begun on the chapel in 1634, when Pietro da Cortona
was commissioned to design the High Altar which was to be the

central feature of the whole chapel. Falconieri apparently soon lost
interest in the scheme and it seems likely that work was never started
on Cortona's design, though it appears from contemporary accounts
that he made a full-size model of it in wood which was installed

in the church. After a long interval, at some date between 1656 and 1664, Falconieri took up the project again, but he entrusted the execution of it to Borromini, in spite of the fact that Cortona was still alive. In his will, dated February 1664, he left instructions that, if the chapel was not finished at the time of his death, his heirs were to carry it to completion. He died a few days later and, when at Borromini's death three years later the work was still unfinished, Falconieri's heirs called upon Ciro Ferri, one of Cortona's most skilful pupils, to complete it. As a result of these various changes of plan it is not easy to distinguish Borromini's contribution to the work as it stands today.

For the High Altar there is a firm starting point, because Cortona's original design survives in a drawing [145], so that it can be compared with the existing structure. At first sight the two designs seem very similar and certain details of Cortona's scheme, such as the group of the Baptism of Christ in sculpture, survive almost unchanged in the present altar, but the modifications which Borromini introduced are in fact crucial. The most important is that he removed the attic with the relief of God the Father which Cortona had inserted between the altar itself and the window above, and continued the columns upwards, thus heightening the whole design and bringing it into closer harmony with the proportions of the church itself. He also made the two outer columns stand forward in relation to the others and replaced Cortona's plain curved pediment with one of his own compound type, at the same time increasing the size of the window which Cortona had planned to have in the field of the pediment, an unusual device for this date. For the red marble columns Borromini used the complex fluting which he had employed on the fireplace of the Sala di Ricreazione of the Oratory. In spite of these changes the altar remains a compromise, since Borromini was not able to eliminate some basic features of Cortona's design which did not really suit his own style. It is, for instance, certain that he would not have chosen to have a group of sculpture as the centre of the altar, but this he was bound to incorporate because it had already been begun by Francesco Mochi, though in fact his group was never set up and the one which now fills the centre of the altar is by Bernini's pupil Antonio Raggi, who, however, has kept surprisingly close to Cortona's original project. The seated statues of Fortitude and Justice on the pediment by Leonardo Reti and the French sculptor Michel Anguier were added after Borromini's death, and it is probably significant that they do not appear in the engraving of the altar given by de' Rossi in his *Disegni di vari*

*altari*, published in 1713, in which their place is taken by two candelabra. The window above the altar has also nothing to do with Borromini but is a variant by Ferri on his master's original design. It
is now filled with disastrous nineteenth-century stained glass.

About the monuments to Falconieri [146] and his brother which
stand against the side walls of the choir we have little certain information, though we know from Falconieri's will that the four green
marble columns were already carved and stood in the Palazzo Fal-

146. S. Giovanni dei Fiorentini, Rome, Falconieri Tomb, after 1656

conieri, and we also learn from one of the early biographers that Borromini was unable to finish the tombs. It is, however, fairly clear from an examination of the monuments themselves which parts are by Borromini and which were added by Ferri after his death. The curvilinear base and the oval niche enclosed by the columns are entirely in accordance with Borromini's later style and are indeed very close in design to the monument to Boniface VIII in the Lateran, but it is inconceivable that, having created this fully three-dimensional structure at the bottom, he should have ended it above with a simple arch entirely in one plane, leaving the columns with nothing to support. Moreover the detail of the upper part is in the idiom used by Cortona and Ferri and bears no likeness to that of Borromini. The effect of the monuments is further falsified by the groups of sculpture at the sides which were added in the eighteenth and nineteenth centuries, though it is clear from the fact that Borromini extended the bases of the tombs beyond the pilasters that he intended to have either figures or perhaps urns or candelabra flanking the main structure. Nothing is known of his intentions for filling the niches, but the existing groups by Ercole Ferrata and Domenico Guidi, which were added after his death, are far from satisfactory and cannot be in accordance with his designs.

From Falconieri's will and from a statement by Martinelli it is certain that Borromini was also involved in the designing of the funerary chapel [147] under the choir of the church, but here again some intervention by Cortona or Ferri seems likely. The form of the chapel, with a dome so low as to be almost flat, is certainly due to Borromini, because a drawing by him exists in the Kunstbibliothek, Berlin, showing the altar and implying the general form of the chapel, but it is far more like Cortona's lower church at SS. Luca e Martina than Borromini's only comparable work, the lower church at S. Carlino, and we may wonder whether Cortona had not made a design for the chapel which Borromini had to take into account. One feature links the chapel with Borromini's later style, namely the use of Doric columns without bases, as at the Collegio di Propaganda Fide, but too much importance should not be attached to this point because the floor of the chapel has certainly been remade, perhaps because of flooding from the Tiber, and it is possible that the bases may have been removed or buried on that occasion. In fact, like all the work carried out for the Falconieri at S. Giovanni dei Fiorentini, the funerary chapel seems to be a compromise between the style of Borromini and that of Cortona and his followers.

147. S. Giovanni dei Fiorentini, Rome, lower chapel, after 1656

One of the most famous works associated with Borromini's name in the last phase of his activity is the Spada Chapel in S. Girolamo della Carità [148]. It has long been evident that this extraordinary creation does not fit stylistically with the architect's late style, and the recently published documents and drawings from the Spada archives prove that in fact he had very little to do with its design and nothing to do with its execution.

The enthusiasm of Virgilio Spada for architecture has been mentioned in connection with the Oratorio di S. Filippo Neri, and the methods adopted by the Spada family generally in the direction

148. S. Girolamo della Carita, Rome, Cappella Spada

of the works which they commissioned have been touched on in relation to the colonnade in the Palazzo Spada. In both these cases
Borromini played a dominant part, but in the case of the Spada
Chapel in S. Girolamo – and in those commissioned by the family
in Faenza and Bologna – it is clear that Virgilio Spada, sometimes
in collaboration with other members of his family, was the directing
spirit, and Borromini was only called in to make a fair copy of an
existing project or sometimes to produce a plan for some detail,
which was almost always altered in execution.

In the case of the earliest of these projects, the family chapel in
the Jesuit church of S. Maria dell'Angelo at Faenza, the designing
and execution of which lasted from about 1631 to 1655, the only
record of Borromini's intervention is a drawing showing the general
design of the High Altar flanked by obelisks, which is almost certainly no more than a fair copy of a scheme worked out by Virgilio
Spada, no doubt with the help of other architects. For the High
Altar of S. Paolo Maggiore two drawings exist for the altar frontal,
clearly invented and drawn by Borromini, but the frontal as executed bears little resemblance to them. A third drawing, for part
of the pavement, is probably again a fair copy of a design by Virgilio
Spada or another architect. In the case of the chapel in S. Girolamo
della Carità a beautiful drawing for the altar frontal from Borromini's own hand exists [149], but only the outer sections bear any
resemblance to what was actually carried out, and these are much

the weakest parts and look as though they were based on the ideas
of another craftsman (or amateur).

The upshot of the new evidence is that, interesting though the
chapel in S. Girolamo is as a fantasy in inlaid marble, which one

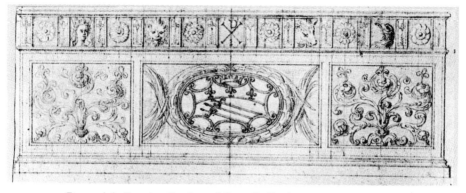

149. Borromini: Drawing for altar of Cappella Spada
in S. Girolamo della Carità, Rome

might expect to see in a Neapolitan rather than a Roman church,
it does not add anything to our understanding of Borromini as an
artist; indeed, it has long been a source of confusion to anyone trying
to determine the architect's style in his late period. Now it can be
seen for what it is, the fantastic invention of a talented amateur
anxious to build a monument to various members of his family and
in a position to call on the advice of a number of professional artists.
The fact that Borromini's share in the creation of the chapel was
so slight is a reflection of the deteriorating relations between the
architect and his patrons. The Spada archives supply vivid and
painful evidence of this situation: letters from one member of the
family to another complaining that it was becoming impossible to
negotiate with him or get him to attend to his work – a repetition
of the complaints about S. Agnese – and, perhaps most significant,
a record of the fact that, when in 1652 Innocent X made Borromini
a *cavaliere* as a reward for his work on the restoration of S. Giovanni
in Laterano, neither the pope nor Prince Camillo Pamphili, who
would normally have replaced him on such an occasion, could face
actually meeting the architect, and arrangements were made for the
cross and the chain of the order to be conveyed to him privately
by Virgilio Spada.

The last years of Borromini's life were a time of great frustration
for him. He was only able to finish one major commission, the Collegio di Propaganda Fide; at S. Andrea delle Fratte and the Cappella

Falconieri he was called in to complete a work begun by another architect, and he did not live to complete either job; moreover, the kind of collaboration which he apparently had to endure with his friend Virgilio Spada must have been artistically difficult and probably painful. It is no wonder that the melancholy of his early years turned into morbid introspection and that he almost cut himself off even from his friends. Added to this he had the bitterness of seeing his rival Bernini gaining greater and greater recognition and carrying off all the best commissions. At one point this feeling of jealousy became so strong that he left Rome and made a journey to Lombardy, probably to his home town, but this remedy was of no effect and on his return his melancholy grew even greater and he spent weeks at a time without going out of the house, 'making new designs for great and fantastic buildings from his imagination and invention'.

The account of his death given by his biographer Lione Pascoli, though highly coloured, is so revealing that it is worth quoting at length:

He had another attack, even more violent, of his hypochondria, which in a few days reduced him to such a state that no one recognized him as Borromini, so distorted was his body and so terrifying his face. He twisted his mouth in a thousand horrible grimaces, and from time to time rolled his eyes in a terrifying manner and sometimes shook and roared like a lion. His nephew consulted doctors, took the advice of friends and called in priests, and all agreed that he must never be left alone so that he should not be allowed any opportunity of hanging himself, and that he must at all costs be made to sleep and so to calm his mind. These were the precise instructions which his nephew gave to the servants and these they carried out. But these measures which were intended to cure his illness aggravated it, because seeing that he was not being obeyed, because he was refused everything that he asked for, and feeling that he was being ill-treated, even if for his own good, his mania became even more intense and his hypochondria changed to an oppression in the chest with symptoms of asthma, and in the end to a sort of continuous frenzy.

Finally, in the early morning of 2 August, in an acute fit of despair he tried to kill himself, but – like Van Gogh – he botched it and lived for some hours, long enough to send for his confessor and to dictate the following account of his suicide:

I have been wounded like this since about half past eight this morning and I will tell you how it happened. I had been feeling ill since the feast of the Magdalene [22 July] and had not been out

on account of my illness except on Saturday and Sunday when I
went to S. Giovanni [dei Fiorentini] for the Jubilee. Last night the
idea came to me of making my will and writing it out with my own
hand, and I began to write it about an hour after supper and I went
on writing with a pencil till about three in the morning. Messer
Francesco Massari my young servant ... who sleeps in the room
next door to look after me and had already gone to bed, seeing that
I was still writing and had not put out the light, called to me, 'Signor
Cavaliere, you ought to put out the light and go to sleep because
it is late and the doctor wants you to sleep.' I replied that I should
have to light the lamp again when I woke up and he answered: 'Put
it out because I'll light it again when you wake up'; and so I stopped
writing, put away the paper on which I had written a little and the
pencil with which I was writing, put out the light and went to sleep.
About five or six I woke up and called to Francesco and told him
to light the lamp, and he answered: 'Signor, no'. And hearing this
reply I suddenly became impatient and began to wonder how I
could do myself some bodily harm, as Francesco had refused to give
me a light; and I remained in that state till about half past eight,
when I remembered that I had a sword in the room at the head
of the bed, hanging among the consecrated candles, and, my impa-
tience at not having a light growing greater, in despair I took the
sword and pulling it out of the scabbard leant the hilt on the bed
and put the point to my side and then fell on it with such force
that it ran into my body, from one side to the other, and in falling
on the sword I fell on to the floor with the sword run through my
body and because of my wound I began to scream, and so Francesco
ran in and opened the window, through which light was coming,
and found me lying on the floor, and he with others whom he had
called pulled the sword out of my side and put me on my bed; and
this is how I came to be wounded.

He asked to be buried in the church of S. Giovanni dei Fiorentini
beside his master Maderno, and among various bequests he gave
five hundred crowns to the servant who had unwittingly caused his
death by obeying his orders too strictly.

There is in this account of his own suicide something infinitely
characteristic of Borromini. To have been under a strain so violent
that it drove him to this act of violence – if not of madness – and
yet immediately afterwards to be able to dictate such a lucid account
of the event, reveals a combination of intense emotional power and
rational detachment which are among the qualities which go to make
him such a great architect.

150. Portrait of Borromini, anonymous engraving

# ※※9※※

# *Influence and Reputation*

Borromini saw himself as the spiritual heir to Michelangelo, and with some reason. None of Michelangelo's immediate successors – with the possible exception of the frustrated Giacomo del Duca – understood the fundamental innovations in his architecture, and none of them developed his discoveries. The history of Roman architecture between about 1565 and 1620 shows a series of cautious developments from Vignola in which occasionally a detail – a door or a window – is incorporated from Michelangelo. Nor did Borromini's contemporaries derive much more sustenance from the study of the great sixteenth-century master. Pietro da Cortona owed much to him in his treatment of the wall, but he never made use of his inventions in planning. Bernini showed something of his feeling for grand scale in his Piazza of St Peter's and borrowed the giant pilasters of the Capitoline Palaces to use them – how timidly! – on the Palazzo Chigi-Odescalchi. The decorative motifs which had been borrowed from Michelangelo by the first generation of Seicento architects passed into the vernacular, but they became more and more commonplace in the process.

Borromini alone really loved Michelangelo's buildings and understood the principles which inspired them: the inventiveness of the planning, the plastic treatment of the wall, the carefully thought-out novelties in the detail, all combined with a profound knowledge of mechanics and skill in construction, so that what seems at first sight to be wilful ingenuity often turns out to be the solution to some practical problem. All these features are to be found in Borromini's buildings as in those of no other of the Roman architects of the Seicento.

But Borromini also saw himself as heir to Michelangelo in a more unfortunate way. As he himself points out, Michelangelo was attacked by more conservative architects for his innovations in the architecture of St Peter's and, although these criticisms were largely due to the jealousy of defeated rivals, they embittered the architect who had already during his long career suffered so many frustrations. With Borromini the case was much worse and the accusations of anarchical breaking of the rules much more violent. From the way in which Martinelli repeatedly emphasizes the fact that Borromini had studied the works of the Ancients, that he understood the principles of architecture laid down by Vitruvius and that he did not want to set up a new school – in other words to bring about a revolution – in architecture, it is evident that accusations to the contrary had been made by his opponents; and this is confirmed by contemporary evidence. Bernini said to Chantelou during his visit to Paris in 1665 that Borromini's architecture was 'extravagant' and that he was 'an ignorant Goth who had corrupted architecture', and he added that 'a painter or a sculptor in their architecture take as their guide to proportion the human body, but Borromini must have based his on chimeras'. Giovanni Pietro Bellori, the spokesman of the classical party in Rome, was even more violent. In his *Idea del pittore, dello scultore, e dell'architetto*, delivered as a lecture in 1664 and published in 1672, he writes:

> ... everyone imagines in his head a new idea or phantom of architecture in his own manner ... so that they deform buildings, even towns and monuments. They use, almost deliriously, angles and broken and distorted lines, they tear apart bases, capitals and columns with crowded stucco decoration and trivial ornaments and with faulty proportions, in spite of the fact that Vitruvius condemns such novelties.

The fact that he does not mention Borromini by name is probably due to a sense of delicacy, because the architect was still alive when Bellori gave his lecture, but there can be no doubt against whom his attack was directed.

Even Borromini's early biographers were apologetic rather than enthusiastic about his achievements and, compared with the warm and unqualified praise which they lavished on Bernini, their comments seem tepid. They are more concerned to talk about his devotion to his art and the unhappiness of his life than to praise his architecture. Giovanni Battista Passeri, writing in the 1670s, sets him up as an illustration of the fact that some artists achieve a reputation in a field for which they had shown no inclination in their youth, Borromini having been trained as a marble-cutter. He goes so far as to describe his architecture as lively (*spiritosa*) and inventive (*ingegnosa*), but immediately adds the qualification, 'if one can forgive a certain capricious irregularity'. A little later in the century Baldinucci, in his biography of Borromini, said that architecture owed much to him and that he exercised this art 'with as much nobility and decorum as any'. Pascoli dwells on the rivalry between Borromini and Bernini but remains carefully non-committal on the qualities of the former, saying that some critics maintained that Borromini 'from a too great desire to introduce novelty into his ornament sometimes broke the rules'. He adds as justification that a certain irregularity is always to be found in nature, but the argument is put forward with little conviction.

The same qualified praise of Borromini, mixed with implied disapproval, is to be found in all the guidebooks to Rome written in the late seventeenth and eighteenth centuries. 'Ingenious', 'capricious', 'singular', 'curious' are the epithets most usually applied, though sometimes the word *vago* ('charming') is added as well. In his *Itinerario istruttivo* of 1777 Giuseppe Vasi speaks of the plan of S. Carlino as 'designed ingeniously and with magnificence in spite of the limited space', but in the 1819 edition he speaks only of Borromini's 'industry' in making the design. The cold wind had started to blow more strongly.

Nor were the practising architects much more understanding. Borromini's own nephew, Bernardo, who had the incalculable advantage of inheriting all his uncle's surviving drawings, seems to have derived no profit from them. He built almost nothing, but he spent a good deal of time producing plans based on his uncle's ideas, always emasculated, however – as, for instance, in the drawings for S. Eustachio – and, what is worse from our point of view, he often ruined his uncle's drawings by working over them in heavy ink lines to produce his own variant, which was never, it is hardly necessary to say, an improvement on the original.

Generally speaking Borromini's influence on Roman architecture in the fifty years after his death is astonishingly slight. Again the parallel with Michelangelo is striking. As was the case with him, architects only made use of Borromini's inventions in the minor features of buildings, not in their general design or conception. The fact that Borromini was replaced at S. Agnese by Carlo Rainaldi was symptomatic of taste in the middle of the century, and Roman architecture in the last quarter of the seventeenth century owes more to him and his contemporary G. A. de Rossi than to Borromini. In the early eighteenth century architects like Passalaqua and Dominicis made some play with Borrominesque ideas of planning in their churches, but in a very timid manner. The façade of S. Maria Maddalena, attributed to Giuseppe Sardi, showed greater originality in the treatment of the forms of window and door pediments, and the same could be said of Gabriele Valvassori in the

Palazzo Doria. Filippo Raguzzini – who was a Sicilian, not a Roman, by birth, it may be noted in passing – put some real vitality into his design for the Piazza in front of S. Ignazio which, though not strictly Borrominesque, is unthinkable without his revolutionary innovations; but not one of these architects dared to develop either the grand complexity of S. Ivo or the concentrated simplicity of Re Magi. What Roman patrons such as Clement XI liked was the respectable, competent, restrained style of Carlo Fontana, who was to have a wider influence on European architecture in the early eighteenth century than either Borromini or Bernini. With the triumph of the 'moderates', Alessandro Galilei and Ferdinando Fuga, in the next generation, the name of Borromini disappears altogether from the history of Roman architecture.

In other parts of Italy Borromini's influence was to be even less marked than in Rome. Each of the great artistic centres was dominated by its particular sixteenth-century hero. Florence was still under the sway of Bernardo Buontalenti, who was one of Michelangelo's ablest followers but one whose interpretation of the master would not allow of any compromise with Borromini's version. Venice was dominated by the principles of Palladio, codified by Vincenzo Scamozzi, and, though Baldassare Longhena evolved a brilliant local Baroque style, it was still conditioned by Palladianism and was as contrary as could be to the methods of Borromini. Genoa still held to the tradition of Galeazzo Alessi; Naples had found its own Baroque in the style of Cosimo Fanzago and was long to remain immune to Roman influence; and Sicily was a law unto itself.

It was only in Turin that Borromini's lessons fell on fruitful ground, in the person of the Theatine brother Guarino Guarini, but even here his influence needs to be carefully defined. Guarini was in Rome for several years from 1639 onwards, that is to say, when Borromini was at work on S. Carlino, the Oratory and S. Ivo, and he learnt much from the study of these buildings, particularly the undulating walls of S. Carlino and S. Ivo, and the interpenetration of ovals and circles of their plans. In the façade of Ste Anne-la-Royale, the Theatine church designed by Guarini for Paris, he borrowed directly from S. Carlino, but generally he interpreted Borromini's ideas in a much more independent manner. The curved walls which enclose the interior of S. Lorenzo at Turin are conceived in the spirit of Borromini, but are quite personal in the way that all four, being on a continuous convex curve, seem to press inwards on the central space. The most fundamental difference between the architecture of the two men is however that, whereas Borromini

conceives his structures entirely in terms of walls and closed vaults
or domes, Guarini covers his churches with a network of ribs with
open spaces between them, through which the eye passes to the
outer shell or sometimes to another network of ribs. At first sight
this method of construction might seem to be derived from Borromini's vaults on the Oratory or Re Magi, but his method is fundamentally different because, as we have seen, Borromini's ribs are
not structural but are simply superimposed on a continuous vault,
whereas Guarini's actually carry the load of the lantern which tops
the cupola. But in his quality of controlled imaginative power
Guarini is the first – perhaps the only – true follower of Borromini
in the late seventeenth century.

He, in his turn, found little understanding in his own country.
His pupil, Bernardo Vittone, who published Guarini's treatise on
architecture after his death, developed his ideas in a brilliantly original way, but the most successful architect of the next generation
in Turin was Filippo Juvarra, a Sicilian by birth and a Roman by
training, who knew the works of Borromini but saw them through
the eyes of Carlo Fontana and his contemporaries. In some of his
smaller villa designs he makes play with combinations of ovals, and
his church towers are often based on Borromini's designs for S.
Agnese, but his churches usually have relatively conventional rectangular or Latin-cross plans, except for the Superga, which is circular. He must rank with Carlo Fontana among the founders of the
international Late Baroque school, which numbers outside Italy
Jules Hardouin-Mansart in France, Fischer von Erlach in Austria,
Conrad Schlaun in Westphalia, Andreas Schlüter in Berlin and
Vanbrugh and Gibbs in England.

At this stage the architectural vocabulary of Borromini became
easily accessible to anyone interested through the publication of the
*Opus* and the *Opera* and the various volumes of engravings produced
by Domenico and Giovanni Giacomo de' Rossi, of which the most
important is the *Studio d'architettura civile*, which appeared between
1702 and 1721. The engravings made available in these publications
gave accurate and detailed renderings of Borromini's designs for
doors, windows and altars, which caught the attention of architects
all over Europe, so that his themes passed into the vernacular of
international architecture; but very few architects studied the plans
which were also provided, and so the essential inventions of Borromini still passed almost unnoticed.

In Central Europe the influence of Borromini was widespread but
less profound than is generally said. The first major foreign architect

to come under the sway of Roman Baroque architecture was the Austrian Johann Bernhard Fischer von Erlach, who spent the years 1670 to 1686 in Rome, but he was much more influenced by Bernini and Carlo Fontana than by Borromini. On his return to Austria, however, he produced a series of brilliant designs for villas and palaces, composed of oval rooms on axes radiating from a single centre at angles of 120°, experiments which would have been unthinkable without the innovation introduced by Borromini, though they are not directly based on any of his works and actually derive more directly – like Juvarra's early projects – from certain rather eccentric unexecuted designs of Carlo Fontana, notably one at Windsor for a villa to be erected in the Veneto. But in his mature works – the Karlskirche, the Hofbibliothek or the Viennese palaces – he developed a grand monumental style, admirably suited to the needs of the Imperial Court, but entirely lacking the freedom and vitality of Borromini's manner. Indeed it owes as much to France, particularly to the work of Louis Le Vau and J. H. Mansart, as to Roman models.

Much has been made of the influence of Borromini, both directly and through Guarini, in Bavaria, Franconia and Bohemia, but here again caution is necessary. In Upper Bavaria the brothers Cosmas Damian and Egid Quirin Asam made frequent use of Borrominesque forms in their windows and doors, and in the forms of their arches, and in the Johann Nepomuk Kirche in Munich the façade and the galleries undulate in a manner directly based on the study of Borromini, though the general effect of the interior, with its rich materials and dramatically directed light, owes more to Bernini than to Borromini. Further, the plans of their churches are generally simple – an unbroken oval at Weltenburg, a near-Greek cross in the Ursulinerinnen at Straubing – and owe nothing to Borromini but go back to traditional sixteenth-century Roman models.

A more direct link with Borromini and Guarini is usually traced in the architecture of Lucas von Hildebrandt in Austria, of the Dientzenhofer family in Bohemia and Franconia, and of Balthasar Neumann in Franconia and the Rhineland. The link undoubtedly exists, and two of Hildebrandt's early churches, S. Lorentz at Gabel in Bohemia and the Piaristenkirche (Maria Treu) in Vienna, are directly based on Guarini's S. Lorenzo in Turin and can therefore be said to have been following, at a second remove, the ideas of Borromini. It has further often been suggested that the complicated vaulting used by the Dientzenhofer family at Woborischt, Prague and Banz, and by Neumann at Würzburg (Hofkirche), Vierzehnheiligen, Neresheim and elsewhere is also derived from Guarini; but in fact it is basically different from his construction. The northern vaults are composed of interlocking domes, that is to say, of continuous thin surfaces composed of brick or sometimes of lath and plaster, in which the lines of intersection of the domes are sometimes marked by the addition of mouldings which make them look like ribs. These 'ribs', however, have no structural function, whereas with Guarini, as has been said, they are the actual elements out of which the vaulting is composed. This form of vaulting seems to derive more directly from a type of late Gothic construction which continued to be used in Bohemia until the early eighteenth century, when it was applied in the strange churches of Giovanni Santini in Prague and elsewhere, which are half Gothic and half Baroque.

In France Borromini's influence on architecture was almost nil, but the decorative designers, such as Meissonnier, adapted many of his forms to their purposes. He is rarely mentioned in the written treatises and, though this silence no doubt means disapproval, the few comments that we find are on the whole surprisingly tolerant. J. F. Blondel, for instance, in his *Cours d'architecture* (V, p. 3) published in 1777, writes:

Il n'y a peut être pas eu un grand mal que Rome ait eu son Borromini, et que nous ayons eu nos Lajoux, nos Meissonnier, nos Pinault; mais il faloit bien laisser leur originalité et non les suivre, comme l'on a fait pendant longtemps.*

The Président de Brosse, who was in Rome in 1739–40, is also moderate. He speaks of the '*jolie architecture*' of S. Carlino and the '*magnificence*' of S. Agnese, though he feels obliged to add in connection with S. Andrea delle Fratte that Borromini 'cannot be defended against the accusation of having created inventions in a bizarre taste'. As would be expected, Lalande, who was in Rome in 1765–6 but did not publish his *Voyage d'Italie* till 1786, is more severe: 'Borromini created a new order of architecture in which curves are combined with straight lines, in a manner which some find ingenious, but of which many architects have disapproved.' English travellers were also generous in their approval, and Edward Wright, who was in Italy in 1720–22, sums up their views in a pretty phrase, saying that in some of his works Borromini 'was a little particular in his fancy, but in the main a great Master'.

---

* 'There was perhaps no great harm in Rome having her Borromini and in our having our Lajoux [Lajoue], our Meissonnier, our Pinault [Pineau]; but it would have been better to leave their originality alone and not to follow their example, as has been done for so long.'

It was, however, from England that the first really savage attacks came. While French architects were moving into the Rococo which, though not directly deriving from Borromini, yet had a freedom in the treatment of classical forms which would have precluded its exponents from being censorious, and while Italy, Austria and South Germany were involved in the last splendid convulsions of the Baroque, England – after a flirtation with the style in the period of Vanbrugh, Hawksmoor and Gibbs – was heading for the severe classicism of the Palladians.*

It is not surprising, therefore, to find that the first great exponent of Palladianism in England, Colen Campbell, should write in the introduction to the *Vitruvius Britannicus*, published in 1715: 'How wildly Extravagant are the Designs of *Borromini*, who has endeavour'd to debauch Mankind with his odd and chimerical Beauties, where the Parts are without Proportion, Solids without their true Bearing, Heaps of Materials without Strength, excessive Ornaments without Grace, and the whole without Symmetry?'; and this was followed up in the middle of the century by Sir William Chambers, who referred to 'the taste of Borromini universally and justly esteemed the most licentious and Extravagant of all modern Italians'.

Later still Henry Swinburne in his *Travels in the Two Sicilies in the years 1777, 1778, 1779 and 1780*, published in 1785, speaks of buildings 'which have been executed upon the plans of Borromini and his scholars' which 'exceed in wanton violation of propriety all the flights of Gothic architecture', and James Barry refers to the *cloacus* (or drain) from which flowed the architecture of 'Borromini and other hairbrained moderns'.

At this stage the Italians joined in the chorus and Francesco Milizia, in his lives of the architects, first published in 1768, writing as the spokesman of neo-classical doctrine, swept Borromini away with a famous condemnation which was copied by lesser writers for generations:

Borromini was one of the first men of his century for the elevation of his genius, but one of the last for the ridiculous use which he made of it. In architecture he was the equivalent of Seneca in litera-

---

* This 'flirtation' is illustrated in a curious document which has recently come to light, namely a design by Rubens for a title-page which the English architect, John Talman, used as the frontispiece of one of his albums of drawings (dismembered after his death); in the blank middle space he wrote:

'A Collection of Altars and Altar Pieces Churches etc. by the famous Boromene etc.' One would like to know what happened to the drawings in the album.

ture and Marino in poetry [two writers who indulged in excessive ingenuity in their style]. In the beginning when he was following others he did well; but when he set up to act on his own, driven on by an uncontrollable urge to surpass Bernini, he slipped, one might say, into heresy. And he elected to achieve excellence by novelty. He did not understand the essentials of architecture. Therefore he abandoned himself to his curvilinear and zig-zag manner of designing and to his great desire for ornament, so contrary to the principles of simplicity; and he gave free rein to his fantasy of using cartouches, curved columns, broken pediments and other extravagant forms. And yet, even in his greatest freaks there is something undefinably grand, harmonious and subtle, which reveals his sublime talent. Now if this genius had only penetrated the secret of architecture; if he had given himself to correct the abuses not recognized by so many far-sighted connoisseurs, blinded by habit; if he had sought true proportions, as yet unrecognized, appropriate to the character of each building, and to improving the members of the orders – which can be improved – then he would have discovered novelties which would have been to the advantage of posterity, and would have surpassed the most remarkable of his predecessors, as well as Bernini. But he took the wrong path, and was the cause that ordinary architects, dazzled by his false brilliance, followed his style, the more clumsily in that they were inferior to him in talent. And so there was the Borrominesque 'sect'. And how can one attack them, the worst of all? Borromini observed precisely all the rules for displeasing the eyes; he was completely insensitive to that part of architecture which concerns beauty and as this part is more important than the others, if one condemns him in this, one condemns him all the more in the others, that is to say commodity and stability in building, in which he was highly skilled. When the true is set next to the false either the latter is rejected or the former is approved. It is a kind of contagion. So difficult is it to distinguish good from bad in a subject. But, unhappily evil is followed and good rejected.

I have quoted this passage at length because it contains the germ of later judgements on Borromini for more than a century – indeed some later writers, such as Quatremère de Quincy, copy Milizia almost verbatim – but these critics differ from Milizia in that whereas he recognized the latent genius of Borromini – however much he condemned its application – they rejected him lock, stock and barrel. A typical example of the nineteenth-century English view of Borromini is that of Joseph Gwilt in his *Encyclopaedia of Architecture*, published in 1881. The passage is too long and rambling to quote in full, but the following extracts will give the flavour of the whole:

He inverted the whole system of Greek and Roman architecture, without replacing it by a substitute ... He formed the project of annihilating all idea of a model, all principles of imitation, all plea for order and proportion. For the restriction in the art ... within the bounds of reason, he substituted the anarchy of imagination and fancy, and an unlimited flight into all species of caprice. Undulating flexibility supplanted all regularity of form; contours of the most grotesque description succeeded to right lines; the severe architrave and entablature were bent to keep up the strange delusion; all species of curves were adopted in his operations, and the angles of his buildings were perplexed with an infinite number of breaks. What makes this pretended system of novelty more absurd is ... that its only novelty was the disorder it introduced, for Borromini did not invent a single form ... he decomposed some, transposed others, and usually employed each member in a situation directly the reverse of its proper place, and, indeed, just where it never would be naturally placed ... With him every thing seems to have gone by contraries; and to give truth the appearance of fiction, and the converse, seems to have been his greatest delight.

At the time Gwilt was writing, however, the rehabilitation of the Baroque began in Central Europe. The first historians to use the word as an art-historical term, as opposed to one of abuse, were Jakob Burckhardt and Wilhelm Lübke, in two works both published in 1885, but neither of these writers showed any special appreciation of Borromini as an architect. However, Gurlitt, in his *Geschichte des Barockstils in Italien*, published in 1887, and Schmarsow, in his *Barock und Rokoko* of 1897, both gave sympathetic analyses of his works. This beginning of appreciation was not, however, followed up, and Wölfflin, the next great exponent of the merits of Baroque art, only mentions Borromini in passing and is much more concerned with Bernini. Even Weisbach, in *Der Barock als Kunst Gegenreformation*, published as late as 1921, does not mention Borromini's name, though he gives him more generous treatment in his volume on the Baroque in the Propyläen History of Art, published three years later; and Brinckmann, in his contribution to the *Handbuch der Kunstwissenschaft*, apparently begun in 1915 but not published till after the First World War, comments on the fact that, though the genius of Bernini was recognized, it was 'still daring' to talk of Borromini or Guarini.

Meanwhile, however, a group of German and Austrian scholars had begun to examine systematically the documents available about Borromini, and this led to a series of articles published just before the first war by Egger, Pollak, Dvořák and others, and to the volumes by Pollak and Orbaan which appeared in the 1920s (the first posthumously) and remain the foundation for all further study of the architect. This movement culminated in the publication in

1924 of Eberhard Hempel's monograph on the architect, which remains the most useful – I had almost written 'the only useful' – book on the subject. It was based on a careful study of all the documents then available – many of them hitherto unpublished – and above all it took full account of the drawings by Borromini in the Albertina. These had been acquired in the early eighteenth century, probably from Bernardo Castello, by Baron Stosch, a friend of Winckelmann, and they represent by far the greater part of the surviving drawings by the artist, though others exist in the Vatican and in the archives of the Oratory. On the basis of all this material Hempel was able to give a clear account of the artist's career, a convincing analysis of his style and an estimate of his achievement which has not been superseded.

In the years between 1924 and the Second World War German scholars did not follow up this beginning and the only work of any significance to be published on Borromini was Hans Sedlmayr's ingenious but perverse analysis of his work in terms of Freudian psychoanalysis (1930).

Other countries were slow to follow the German lead in the study of Borromini. In England nothing was written about him by architectural historians, though Osbert and Sacheverell Sitwell gave him a few sentences of appreciation in their books touching on the Baroque. Some younger students were in fact engaged in studying the architect, but nothing appeared in print.

Meanwhile the attitude of the English towards the Baroque in general was profoundly affected by the arrival in this country of German architectural historians, particularly the late Rudolf Wittkower and Sir Nikolaus Pevsner. Wittkower's article 'Carlo Rainaldi and the Roman architecture of the full Baroque', published in the *Art Bulletin* for 1937, was the first statement in English of the importance of Borromini as an architect and the first analysis of his style in relation to that of Bernini and other architects of the Roman Baroque. Pevsner, in his *History of European Architecture*, published in 1942, gave a short general account of Borromini's achievement, and Wittkower came back to the subject in his masterly chapter on the architect in his volume in the Pelican History of Art (1958).

Italian scholars were surprisingly slow in joining in the 'discovery' of their great compatriot. Up to the time of the Second World War they had produced nothing more than a few articles and pamphlets, but since 1945 the fashion for books on Borromini has spread. Argan's short monograph, published in 1952, gives a brilliant but tortuous analysis of Borromini's artistic personality, but the most prolific exponent of Borromini's merits is Professor Paolo Portoghesi, whose two generously illustrated books, published in 1964 and 1967, were the first since Hempel's to cover the artist's career in detail.

During the same period, however, the scholarly study of Borromini had developed with real seriousness. An international team of scholars – Italian, German, American, Swedish, Danish and English – took up again the search for archives initiated fifty years earlier, began a systematic study of the drawings and re-examined individual buildings. The result of this research has been a series of studies which have greatly widened our knowledge of Borromini's individual buildings and of his methods of work. This work reached a climax in 1967, the tercentenary of Borromini's death, when congresses and commemorative exhibitions were held, the results of which were recorded in a series of important publications. Research on Borromini continues and many scholars are now engaged in carrying on the work of the pioneers.

To end with a query on this great and enigmatic architect, the depths of whose genius will never be plumbed: why, after three centuries of neglect or abuse, has Borromini suddenly come to receive such intense and widespread admiration? What are the qualities in his art which appeal so intensely to students of architecture in the mid-twentieth century?

The question is not easy to answer. Certain negative factors are clear. We are no longer prejudiced against him by the belief that all architecture should be based on the principles of Vitruvius, or that the only truly religious architecture is that of the Middle Ages. Further it is reasonable that for an age which has produced Le Corbusier on the one hand and Nervi on the other there should be a particular fascination in the mathematical precision and the structural fantasy of Borromini. But there is more to it than that. We appreciate a struggle between opposites, not, as the Romantics did, in the expectation of defeat, but in the hope that a synthesis will be achieved. To us the struggle in Borromini between imaginative energy and intellectual control can be more attractive than the easy achievement of Bernini's rhetoric. It may well be that in more relaxed periods Bernini's art will once more have the greater appeal, but in the meanwhile the intense passion of Borromini – though it led him to suicide – can give us greater satisfaction.

# Notes on Further Reading

The earliest printed biographies of Borromini are those by Giovanni Battista Passeri, Filippo Baldinucci and Lione Pascoli. Passeri's *Vite de' pittori, scultori ed architetti* was not published till 1772, but the original manuscript, written in the 1670s, was printed with elaborate notes by J. Hess under the title *Die Künstlerbiographien des Giovanni Battista Passeri*, Vienna–Leipzig, 1934. Baldinucci's appeared in the fifth volume of his *Notizie de' professori del disegno*, published in 1728. Pascoli's is in the first volume of the *Vite de' pittori, scultori ed architetti moderni*, Rome, 1730. Baldinucci drew heavily on a manuscript life in the Biblioteca Nazionale in Florence (Codex Magliabecchianus II. II., 110 ff., fols. 170ʳ–171ᵛ), which was almost certainly written by the architect's nephew, Bernardo (cf. R. Wittkower, in *Studi sul Borromini*, Accademia di San Luca, Rome, 1967, I, 34 ff.). Of the three printed biographies Baldinucci's is the most reliable and Pascoli's the fullest. Passeri adds a few details not mentioned by the other biographers, but he is wrong on several points about Borromini's early life, particularly in stating that he reached Rome in 1624.

Much information can be gleaned from the early guidebooks to Rome, of which a complete bibliography is given by L. Schudt in *Le guide di Roma*, Vienna–Augsburg, 1930. The most important is *Roma ornata dell' architettura, pittura e scoltura*, written by Borromini's friend, Fioravante Martinelli, of which the manuscript, written about 1660–62, was published by Cesare d'Onofrio under the title *Roma nel Seicento*, Florence, 1969. It is a much enlarged version of his *Roma ricercata nel suo sito*, first printed in 1644 and often republished, but the manuscript printed by Cesare d'Onofrio is of far greater interest and contains long passages inspired by Borromini himself, who also made marginal notes in the manuscript. A few notes of interest are to be found in G. B. Mola, *Breve racconto delle miglior opere d'architettura, scultura et pittura fatte in Roma*, written in 1663 and published by K. Noehles, Berlin, 1966, under the title *Roma l'anno 1663 di Giov. Batt. Mola*.

The most important documents about Borromini are to be found in O. Pollak, *Die Kunsttätigkeit unter Urban VIII*, Vienna, 1928 and 1931, which unfortunately, as its title implies, only covers the period up to 1644. A number of other documents were shown at a tercentenary exhibition organized by the Archivio di Stato of Rome in 1967 and shown in the Biblioteca Alessandrina in the Sapienza. These are recorded in an admirable catalogue by Marcello del Piazzo, entitled *Ragguagli Borrominiani*, Rome, 1968, which provides by far the fullest documentation for Borromini's career. Other documents will be referred to in the sections dealing with individual buildings.

The drawings are being published by Heinrich Thelen, but so far only the first volume of his catalogue has appeared (*Francesco Borromini. Die Handzeichnungen*, Graz, 1967), covering the period up to about 1630. It deals with the drawings made under Maderno and Bernini, principally those for St Peter's, S. Ignazio, the Pantheon and the Palazzo Barberini, but it also includes the copies of fragments of ancient architecture made by Borromini after the Codex Coner. The book contains an astonishing amount of information, but some of the author's conclusions are open to doubt (cf. the present writer's review in *Kunstchronik*, XXII, 1969, 89–93). The drawings in the Vatican Library were exhibited in 1967, with a catalogue also by Thelen (*Francesco Borromini. Disegni e documenti Vaticani*, Vatican, 1967), which includes valuable information about Borromini himself and also about the other architects involved in schemes on which he worked. Seventy drawings from the Albertina in Vienna, where the greater part of the architect's drawings are preserved, were shown at the Farnesina, Rome, in 1958, with a brief catalogue by Thelen (*70 disegni di F. Borromini delle collezioni dell'Albertina*, Rome, 1958).

Engravings mainly made under Borromini's direction of two of his most important works were published after his death in two volumes, the *Opera del Cavaliere Borromini*, Rome, 1720, covering the Sapienza, and the *Opus architectonicum*, Rome, 1725, covering the Oratory of S. Filippo Neri. The latter has important text prepared by Virgilio Spada from information supplied by Borromini himself and written under his name, which should be read in conjunction with a dialogue written by Spada under his own name, covering much of the same ground (Incisa della Rocchetta, 'Un dialogo del P. Virgilio Spada', *Archivio della Società Romana di Storia Patria*, XC, 1967, 165 ff.). The *Opera* and the *Opus architectonicum* were reprinted in slightly reduced format by the Gregg Press in 1965. It is sometimes said that the engravings in these two volumes are not true to Borromini's intentions and that in some cases they include, for instance, geometrical schemes due to the engraver, but where a comparison can be made with the original drawing, as in the case of Illustration 89, the engraving corresponds accurately to it. Other useful engravings, particularly of details such as altars, doors and windows, are to be found in Domenico de' Rossi's *Studio d'architettura civile*, Rome, 1702–21, Giovanni Giacomo de' Rossi's *Disegni di vari altari e cappelle*, Rome, 1713, and *Insignium Romae templorum prospectus*, Rome, 1680. All but the last of these have been reprinted by the Gregg Press in 1972.

For the general history of Roman Baroque architecture much the most valuable book is Wittkower's volume in the Pelican History of Art, *Art and Architecture in Italy 1600–1750* (3rd edition, 1973). Portoghesi's *Roma barocca* (American translation, Cambridge, Mass., 1970) contains brilliant but misleading photographs of the most famous buildings and also of many of the less well known works of the late seventeenth and early eighteenth centuries. Hibbard (*Carlo Maderno*, London, 1972) gives an excellent account of the immediately preceding period, roughly 1570 to 1620.

The most useful general book on Borromini is still E. Hempel's *Francesco Borromini*, Vienna, 1924, in German (an Italian translation appeared in 1926, and a revised German edition in 1939), based on a careful study of the documents and drawings then available, with a good selection of plates reproduced in rather lifeless half-tone. The most penetrating analysis of Borromini's architecture is given in Rudolf Wittkower's volume in the Pelican History of Art referred to above. Hans Sedlmayr's essay, *Die Architektur Borrominis*, Berlin, 1930, is only recommended to those who have a taste for the extremely alembicated Viennese type of art history current in the 1920s. G. C. Argan's *Francesco Borromini*, Verona, 1952, is brilliant but also difficult for an English reader. The most popular recent book is Paolo Portoghesi's *Borromini. Architettura come linguaggio*, Milan, 1967 (American translation, *The Rome of Borromini*, New York, 1968), which reproduces a number of otherwise unpublished drawings in the Albertina. The text, however, is based, as the title implies, on an analogy between architecture and grammar which to the English mind is hard to follow, and the photographs of buildings reproduced, while brilliant as photographs, often falsify the effect of the originals. The same author produced a series of articles on Borromini which were reprinted in the much more useful *Borromini nella cultura europea*, Rome,

1964. A brief but sensible and well-illustrated book on the architect is P. Bianconi's *Francesco Borromini*, Bellinzona, 1967. The tercentenary of Borromini's death was celebrated in 1967 by a congress organized by the Accademia Nazionale di S. Luca in Rome, the acts of which, published under the title *Studi sul Borromini*, Rome, 1970–72, contain several papers of importance. Rudolf Wittkower gave the opening lecture, entitled *Francesco Borromini: Personalità e destino*, in which he gives a balanced view on the problem of Borromini's psychological make-up, to which are attached in the printed version valuable appendices, including one on the connection of Borromini's ideas with Stoicism. An English version of this paper is printed in the volume of essays published posthumously, entitled *Studies in the Italian Baroque*, London, 1975. Other useful papers in the two volumes of the *Studi* are E. Battisti's essay on *Il simbolismo in Borromini*, and R. Pacini's on *Alterazioni dei monumenti borrominiani*, which records the restoration and alterations which have been carried out on Borromini's buildings in the last hundred years.

CHAPTER I: BIRTH AND EARLY TRAINING (*pages 13–25*)

Apart from the accounts given of Borromini in the general books quoted above, particularly Thelen's *Handzeichnungen*, the most useful information about his early career is to be found in H. Hibbard's *Carlo Maderno*, London, 1972, which provides important dates, clears up a number of points on the relationship between master and pupil and defines, as far as is possible, Borromini's share in their joint undertakings. The section of this book dealing with the Palazzo Barberini supersedes the present writer's article on the subject in the *Journal of the Warburg and Courtauld Institutes* for 1958, 256 ff. For the Fontana delle Api, see H. Hibbard and E. Jaffé, 'Bernini's "Barcaccia"', *Burlington Magazine*, CVI, 1964, 16 f.

For the buildings which Borromini may have seen in Lombardy before coming to Rome, particularly those of Ricchino, see L. Grassi, *Province del Barocco e del Rococò. Lessico di architetti in Lombardia*, Milan, 1966. For S. Lucia in Selci, see Portoghesi, *Borromini nella cultura europea*, 205 ff., and Hibbard, *Carlo Maderno*, 136 ff. The documents about the dome of S. Andrea della Valle are given in *Ragguagli*, 75. For the complicated question of Borromini's share in the Baldacchino and the other work directed by Bernini in St Peter's, see Thelen, *Handzeichnungen* and *Zur Entstehungsgeschichte der Hochaltar-Architektur von St Peter in Rom*, Berlin, 1967, both in difficult German; I. Lavin, *Bernini and the Crossing of Saint Peter's*, New York, 1968, and J. Montagu's review of Thelen in the *Art Quarterly*, XXXIV, 1971, 290 ff.

It was probably while he was working under Maderno that Borromini made drawings for the two towers added to the Pantheon, which are generally attributed to Bernini (cf. T. Thieme, 'Disegni di cantiere per i campanili del Pantheon. Graffiti sui marmi della copertura', *Palladio*, N.S. XX, 1970, 73). The drawings are reproduced in Thelen, *Handzeichnungen*, C 26, 27.

The documents about the manslaughter at the Lateran are given in A. Bertolotti, *Artisti Lombardi a Roma*, Bologna, 1881, II, 32 ff. For the origin of the name Borromini, see Wittkower, *Studies in the Italian Baroque*, London, 1975, 158. I cannot, however, accept Wittkower's suggestion that the name was intended to incorporate a reference to Bernini, a sort of elided form of Borromeo–Bernini.

CHAPTER 2: SOURCES AND THEORIES (*pages 26–51*)

All the books on Borromini mentioned in the first part of the bibliography contain analyses of his ideas on architecture, not always either succinct or convincing.

The evidence about his attitude towards antiquity is to be found in his statements in the *Opus architectonicum* and in Martinelli. For the passages about the Golden House of Nero, see Thelen, *Francesco Borromini, Mostra di disegni e documenti Vaticani*, Rome, 1967, 10. The drawing of the Licinian Garden is reproduced in *Ragguagli* (pl. XLVIII) and that for the restoration of the pyramid of Caius Cestius in M. Fagiolo dell'Arco, 'La religiosa trasmutazione della piramide di Caio Sestio', *Arte illustrata*, V, 1972, 210. For a general discussion of Borromini's relation to antiquity and his use of Montano's drawings, see the present writer's paper in *Studies in Western Art. Acts of the Twentieth Congress of History of Art, New York 1961*, Princeton, 1963, III, 3 ff.

Margaret Lyttelton, in her *Baroque Architecture in Classical Antiquity*, London, 1974, gives a useful account and good plates of the kind of ancient architecture most closely related to Roman seventeenth-century Baroque. For some further discussion of how far Borromini and his contemporaries may have known the architecture of the Eastern Empire, see the present author's review of her book (*Burlington Magazine*, CXVII, 1975, 320 ff.).

### CHAPTER 3: S. CARLO ALLE QUATTRO FONTANE (*pages 52–84*)

The documents about S. Carlo alle Quattro Fontane are published in Pollak (*Die Kunsttätigkeit*, 36 ff.), but a few were added in *Ragguagli* (82 ff., 205 ff.). Most of the available drawings are published by Portoghesi (*Borromini*, 1969, pls. V–XXIX). The three drawings published by Hempel (*Francesco Borromini*, figs. 6, 7, 9) as preliminary studies for S. Carlino were proved by Professor Leo Steinberg in his thesis *San Carlo alle Quattro Fontane. A Study in Multiple Form and Architectural Symbolism*, New York, 1977, to be certainly not connected with the church and probably not by Borromini. For a discussion of the drawings actually connected with the church and also for the problems connected with the façade, see the present writer's review of Portoghesi's *Borromini* (*Burlington Magazine*, CXIII, 1971, 670 ff.). Measured drawings of the cloister are given by A. Contri, 'S. Carlino alle Quattro Fontane (Il chiostro di Francesco Borromini)', *Architettura*, I, 1955, 219 ff. By far the most detailed analysis of the church is to be found in Professor Steinberg's thesis quoted above. A volume of the *Tesori d'arte* series contains a survey of the building history and some good plates. For the problem of the composite capitals with inverted scrolls used by Borromini in S. Carlino, see I. Bee, 'Il capitello compositi a volute invertite. Saggio su una forma antica nella struttura borrominiana', *Analecta romana instituti danici*, VI, 1971, 226 f.

For a discussion of the oval church before S. Carlino, see W. Lotz, 'Die ovalen Kirchenräume des Cinquecento', *Römisches Jahrbuch für Kunstgeschichté*, VII, 1955, 7 ff.

### CHAPTER 4: THE ORATORY OF S. FILIPPO NERI
### AND THE FILOMARINO ALTAR (*pages 85–110*)

The history of the Oratorio di S. Filippo Neri is more fully documented than any other work by Borromini, but the documents are now scattered in various Roman libraries. The most important source is the series of *Decreti* preserved in the archives of the Congretation at the Oratory itself, which cover the whole period of building activity and record every decision of importance in relation to the planning, the actual building and the appointment, dismissal or withdrawal of the architects involved. The actual payments are recorded in the *Libri mastri*, which are now in the Archivio di Stato (Congregazione dell' Oratorio, vols. 371,

372). Extremely important additional information is to be found in various papers by Virgilio Spada. The archives of the Oratory preserve his manuscript of the *Opus architectonicum* with drawings connected with the whole building of the Oratory, including plans by Maruscelli and others for the whole complex, and also a dialogue on the building (Archivio Vallicelliano C. II. 7, ff. 1–16) which corresponds in great part to the *Opus* but contains new information. A further manuscript by Spada, now in the Biblioteca Vallicelliana (o57(2), 48), contains a number of drawings relevant to the Oratory. A great part of this material has been published. The *Opus architectonicum* was printed in Rome in 1725 with sixty-seven folio engravings of the Oratory. The relevant documents from the *Libri mastri* up to 1644 are printed in Pollak (*Die Kunsttätigkeit*, 423 ff.), and those from 1645 to 1651 in A. Pernier, 'Documenti inediti sopra un'opera del Borromini. La fabbrica dei Filippini a Monte Giordano', *Archivi d'Italia*, Second Series, II, 1935, 204 ff. Virgilio Spada's dialogue was published by the Marchese Giovanni Incisa della Rocchetta ('Un dialogo del P. Virgilio Spada', *Archivio della Società Romana di Storia Patria*, XC, 1967, 165 ff.), who also gives valuable quotations from the *Decreti* of the Congregation. The *Decreti* were used by Hempel, but he does not seem to have studied them carefully, and his account of the building history is consequently incomplete and in some respects misleading.

For the room of S. Filippo Neri and the chapels connected with it, the fundamental article is A. Bruschi, 'Il Borromini nelle Stanze di S. Filippo alla Vallicella' (*Palatino*, XII, 1968, 13 ff.), but useful photographs of this part of the building, as well as of the Sacristy and Oratory itself, are to be found in the volume dealing with the church of S. Maria in Vallicella in the *Tesori d'arte cristiana* (no. 93). For a general account of the building, see G. Incisa della Rocchetta, *L'Oratorio borrominiano* (Quaderni dell'Oratorio, 13, 1967). Carlo Gastarri's *L'Oratorio romano dal Cinquecento al Novecento*, Rome, 1962, gives the fullest available history of the order. For an account of Virgilio Spada and his papers in the Vatican (Vat. Lat. 11257, 11258), see F. Ehrle, 'Dalle carte e dai disegni di Virgilio Spada', *Memorie della Ponteficia Accademia Romana di Archeologia*, Series III, II, 1926, 1 ff. Dr Joseph Connors's thesis on the Oratory for a Ph.D. at Princeton will bring together all the available evidence about the Oratory, will add much new material and will give new and important interpretations. His discoveries about the early history of the building and particularly about the share of Maruscelli have been published in an article, 'Early Projects for the Casa dei Filippini in Rome', *Oratorium*, VI, 1975, 107 ff.

The documents for the Filomarino altar are published in the *Ragguagli* (97 f.), and in G. Doria and F. Bologna's catalogue of the *Mostra del ritratto storico napoletano*, held in the Palazzo Reale, Naples, in 1954 (105 f.). The passage about the Cappella del Tesoro is transcribed by L. Montalto, 'Le probleme della cupola di S. Ignazio di Padre Orazio Grassi', *Bollettino del Centro di Studi per la Storia dell'Architettura*, XI, 1957, 46. Further details about the origin of the project are given in Carlo Celano's *Delle notizie del bello dell'antico e del curioso nella città di Napoli*, Naples, 1692 (reprinted with additions by Chiarini, Naples, 1856–60, II, 619 ff.).

Martinelli (p. 14) states that 'l'ornamento della tribuna con colonnato' in S. Anastasia was designed by Borromini and was commissioned by Cardinal Ulderico Carpegna, who was titular cardinal of the church from 1633 to 1659. Martinelli's statement probably refers to the six columns which were added at an unknown date to the ciborium of the High Altar (set up in 1585 by Cardinal Capano but later removed; cf. G. M. Crescimbeni, *L'Istoria della Basilica di S. Anastasia*, Rome, 1722, 19). Nothing seems now to survive of Borromini's work in the church.

The documents about the building of S. Ivo and the completion of the Sapienza are mainly printed in Pollak (*Die Kunsttätigkeit*, I, 159 ff.) and the *Ragguagli* (131 ff., 225 ff.). The engravings appear in the *Opera*, which has a short preface. The drawings are reproduced by Hempel and Portoghesi (*Borromini* and *Borromini nella cultura europea*). For an analysis of the subtle irregularities in the geometry of the church, see Benevolo, 'Il tempo geometrico di S. Ivo della Sapienza', *Quaderni dell'Istituto di Storia dell'Architettura dell'Università di Roma*, 3, 1953, 1 ff. The symbolism of the church is discussed in H. Ost, 'Borrominis römische Universitätskirche', *Zeitschrift für Kunstgeschichte*, XXX, 1967, 101 ff.; P. de la Ruffinière du Prey, 'Salomonic Symbolism in Borromini's Church of S. Ivo della Sapienza', *ibid.*, XXXI, 1968, 216 ff. (based on a lecture by the present writer); E. Battisti, 'Il simbolismo in Borromini', *Studi sul Borromini*, I, 1967, 231 ff., and W. Hauptman, 'Luceat Lux Vestra coram Hominibus: A New Source for the Spire of Borromini', *Journal of the Society of Architectural Historians*, XXXIII, 1974, 73 ff. Borromini's note about the structure of the dome is published in *Ragguagli*, I, 151. Thelen ('Der Palazzo della Sapienza in Rom', *Miscellanea Bibliothecae Hertzianae*, Vienna, 1961, 285 ff.) gives the best account of the earlier history of the building of the Sapienza and shows its exact state when Borromini began work. For the question of the pavement of the church, see Benevolo, 'Il problema dei pavimenti borrominiani in bianco e nero', *Quaderni dell'Istituto di Storia dell'Architettura*, 13, 1956, 1 ff.

Drawings showing della Porta's plans for a round church at the end of the courtyard were found by J. Wasserman, 'Giacomo della Porta's Church for the Sapienza in Rome', *Art Bulletin*, XLVI, 1966, 501 ff. The drawing with the bee-symbolism and the seven columns round the High Altar is partly reproduced by Portoghesi, *Borromini nella cultura europea*, pl. 58. The hidden light source is described in a report that derives from Borromini himself (*Ragguagli*, 227); the dates when the window was altered were discovered by Pacini ('Alterazioni dei monumenti Borrominiani', *Ragguagli*, I, 315). The full-sized autograph drawings found on the library walls are reproduced in E. Re, *Biblioteca alessandrina*, Rome, n.d., 11 f., and Portoghesi, *Borromini nella cultura europea*, fig. 72.

For S. Maria dei Sette Dolori, see Mario Bosi, *S. Maria dei Sette Dolori* (Chiese di Roma, no. 117), Rome, 1971. Measured drawings are given in Perugini, *Architettura di Borromini nella chiesa di S. Maria dei Sette Dolori*, Rome, 1959–60.

CHAPTER 6 : S. GIOVANNI IN LATERANO
AND S. AGNESE IN PIAZZA NAVONA *(pages 133–60)*

For the question of the towers of St Peter's, see Fraschetti, *Il Bernini*, Milan, 1900, 161 ff.; Brauer und Wittkower, *Die Zeichnungen des Gianlorenzo Bernini*, Berlin, 1931, 37 ff.; and Henry Millon, 'An Early Seventeenth Century Drawing of the Piazza San Pietro', *Art Quarterly*, 1962, 229 ff. For a survey of the problem, see H. Hibbard, *Bernini*, Harmondsworth, 1965. Borromini's drawings for the towers are published by Hempel, but see also Thelen, *Mostra di disegni e documenti vaticani*, 14.

For the Lateran the most reliable general account is that of Hempel, who reproduces the essential drawings and gives a summary of the information contained in C. Rasponi, *De Basilica et Patriarcha Lateranensi*, Rome, 1656. A few documents are added in *Ragguagli* (109 ff.), and Martinelli gives an important account of the reasons why Borromini was chosen for the job of restoring the basilica in the *Primo trofeo della Santissima Croce*, Rome, 1655, 131 ff. Some of the early articles on the restoration of the church are still of interest, particularly H. Egger's 'Francesco Borromini's Umbau von S. Giovanni in Laterano', *Beiträge zur Kunstgeschichte Franz Wickhoff gewidmet*, Vienna, 1903, 134 ff.; and Dvořák's 'Francesco Borromini als Restaurator', *Kunstgeschichtliches Jahrbuch der preussischen Kunstsammlungen*, XLII, 1921, 55 ff. For the question of Borromini's intention to vault the basilica, see Thelen, 'Zur barocken Umgestaltung des Langhauses der Lateran Basilika', *Kunstchronik*, VII, 1954, 264 f. Marcello Fagiolo ('Borromini in Laterano. Il nuovo tempio per il concilio universale', *L'arte*, N.S. IV, 1971, 4 ff.) analyses the symbolism of the project. For the original form of the church, in particular the arrangement of 'stepped' aisles, see Krautheimer, *Rivista di archeologia cristiana*, XLIII, 1967, 124 ff.

Borromini's tombs in the Lateran and the drawings for them are reproduced by Hempel and Portoghesi (*Borromini nella cultura europea*).

For the tomb of Cardinal Ceva, see A. Schiavo, 'Un'opera del Borromini nella Cappella Lateranense di S. Venanzio', *Studi romani*, XVI, 1968, 344. The documents about Ceva's plans for the Noviciate of the Jesuits are referred to by F. Haskell, *Patrons and Painters*, London, 1963, 861. The Merlini tomb is discussed by Portoghesi (op. cit., 52), who wrongly attributes the drawings connected with it to Borromini. M. Heimbürger ('Un'disegno certo dell'Algardi e alcuni probabili da Gregorio Spada', *Paragone*, 257, 1969, 57 ff.) ascribes them convincingly to Gregorio Spada, brother of Virgilio. She further points out that the Merlini tomb and that of Giordano Manili which stands opposite it are both shown in Spada's drawings, and that both must have been designed simultaneously, whereas most writers have assumed that the Manili tomb was earlier. Martinelli ascribes the Merlini tomb to Borromini, but it is unlikely that he did more than give advice on the project and perhaps suggest alterations. The tomb is quite unlike Borromini's certain works.

A full and detailed account of the complicated story of the building of S. Agnese in Piazza Navona and the Palazzo Pamphili is given by G. Eimer, *La Fabbrica di S. Agnese in Navona*, Stockholm, 1970–71. Some of the most important documents are given in Montalto, 'Il drammatico licenziamento di Francesco Borromini dalla fabbrica di S. Agnese in Agone', *Palladio*, N.S. VIII, 1958, 129 ff. The intervention of Bernini in the building of the church is described by Preimesberger in 'Bernini a S. Agnese in Agone', *Colloqui del Sodalizio*, Series 3, 1970–72, 44. (This rare publication is available in the library of the Warburg Institute, London.)

CHAPTER 7 : DOMESTIC ARCHITECTURE (*pages 161–82*)

For the Palazzo Carpegna, see M. Tafuri, 'Borromini in Palazzo Carpegna', *Quaderni dell'Istituto di Storia dell'Architettura*, 14, 1957, 85 ff.

For the Palazzo Falconieri Pollak's essay ('Die Decken des Palazzo Falconieri', *Kunstgeschichtliches Jahrbuch der KK. Zentral-Kommission*, V, 1911, 112 ff.) is still useful. Better plates are available in Portoghesi's *Borromini nella cultura europea*. For the symbolism of the ceilings, see Battisti in *Studi sul Borromini*, I, 231 ff. Additional drawings and documents are given by Tafuri in L. Salerno, L. Spezzaferro and M. Tafuri, *Via Giulia*, Rome, 1973, 445 ff.

Those in the Kunstbibliothek, Berlin, are published by H. Thelen in the catalogue of the exhibition *Fünf Architekten aus fünf Jahrhunderten*, held there in 1976 (27 ff.). A photograph of the destroyed chapel of the palace was discovered by Thelen and also by Elizabeth G. Howard, who published it in the *Burlington Magazine* (CXIX, 1977, 31). This discovery made it possible to identify certain drawings as being for the ceiling of the chapel.

Good plates of the interior of the Palazzo Pamphili are to be found in A. Amadei, 'Il Palazzo Pamphili in Piazza Navona', *Capitolium*, XXXVI, 1961, 18 ff.

O. Pollak in his article, 'Antonio del Grande' (*Kunstgeschichtliches Jahrbuch der KK. Zentral-Kommission*, III, 1909, 133 ff.) attributes the seventeenth-century remodelling of the Palazzo di Spagna to Antonio del Grande, but his conclusion is based on a misinterpretation of the evidence, and Borromini's own statement in the *Opus architectonicum* to the effect that he designed the staircase – and therefore probably the vestibule – must be accepted.

For the Palazzo Giustiniani, see I. Toesca, 'Note sulla storia del Palazzo Giustiniani a San Luigi dei Francesi', *Bollettino d'arte*, XLII, 1957, 296 ff.

For the Palazzo di S. Spirito, see M. Heimbürger-Ravalli, 'Disegni sconosciuti del Borromini per il Banco di Santo Spirito', *Paragone*, XXI, 1973, no. 275, 57 ff.

For the few known facts about the Casino del Bufalo, see R. Kultzen, 'Die Malereien Polidoro da Caravaggios im Giardino del Bufalo', *Mitteilungen des Kunsthistorischen Instituts, Florenz*, 1960, 99 ff.

For Palazzo Spada see L. Neppi, *Palazzo Spada*, Rome, 1975, and M. Heimbürger-Ravalli, *Architettura, scultura e arti minori nel Barocco; ricerche nell'archivio Spada*, Florence, 1977, 118 ff. The two authors publish documents from the Spada archives which date the colonnade to 1652–3 and provide important information about the share of Borromini in the work on the palace.

### CHAPTER 8: THE LAST PHASE (*pages 183–209*)

For the history of the Collegio di Propaganda Fide, see G. Antonazzi, 'La sede della Sacra Congregazione e del Collegio Urbano', *Sacrae congregationis de propaganda fide memoria rerum*, ed. J. Meller, Rome, 1971, I, 306 ff. For S. Andrea delle Fratte, see M. d'Onofrio, *S. Andrea delle Fratte* (Chiese di Roma, no. 116), Rome, 1971. For S. Giovanni in Oleo, see Mattiae *et al.*, *S. Giovanni a Porta Latina* (Chiese di Roma, no. 51), Rome, n.d., and M. L. Polidori, *Monumenti e mecenati francesi in Roma*, Viterbo, 1969. For the Falconieri chapels and tombs in S. Giovanni dei Fiorentini, see K. Noehles, *La chiesa dei SS. Luca e Martina*, Rome, 1970, 13, 29, and Luigi Salerno, Luigi Spezzaferro and Manfredo Tafuri, *La Via Giulia*, Rome, 1973, 224 ff.

For the various Spada chapels see M. Heimbürger-Ravalli, *Architettura, scultura e arti minori nel Barocco; ricerche nell'archivio Spada*, Florence, 1977, 75 ff.

# List of Illustrations

The Courtauld Institute of Art has been abbreviated to C.I.A.

26. Piranesi: Ancient Roman tomb near Capua, called the Conocchia (C.I.A.)
27. Temple of Apollo Sosianus, Rome, base of column, drawing from Codex Coner of the early sixteenth century. *Sir John Soane's Museum, London* (C.I.A.)
28. El Deir, Petra (Manoug)
29. Temple of Venus, Baalbek (C.I.A.)
30. Borromini: S. Ivo della Sapienza, Rome, plan of lantern, engraving (From Borromini, *Opera*, 1720)
31. Borromini: Oratorio di S. Filippo Neri, detail of fireplace in Sala di Ricreazione (C.I.A.)
32. G. B. Montano: Roman columns, detail of drawing. *Sir John Soane's Museum, London* (C.I.A.)
33. G. B. Montano: Reconstruction of an ancient Roman building, engraving (From *Li cinque libri di architettura*, 1691)
34. G. B. Montano: Reconstruction of an ancient Roman building, engraving (From *Li cinque libri di architettura*, 1691)
35. Borromini: Palazzo Spada, Rome, colonnade (C.I.A.)
36. Borromini: Palazzo Spada, Rome, colonnade, plan (Redrawn by Julian Bishop)
37. Roman relief. *Uffizi, Florence* (Alinari)
38. Borromini: S. Carlo alle Quattro Fontane, Rome, plan, 1634–41 (From Hempel, *Borromini*, fig. 5)
39. Borromini: S. Carlo alle Quattro Fontane, Rome, diagram of plan (After Sedlmayr, *Die Architektur Borrominis*, redrawn by Julian Bishop)
40. Borromini: Drawings for a fountain for the Oratorio di S. Filippo Neri, Rome. *Albertina, Vienna, 336* (C.I.A.)
41. Lieven Cruyl: View of Quattro Fontane, Rome, with S. Carlo on extreme left, drawing, 1665 (After Egger, *Römische Veduten*; C.I.A.)
42. Borromini: S. Carlo alle Quattro Fontane, Rome, old refectory, now sacristy, 1634–7 (C.I.A.)
43. Borromini: S. Carlo alle Quattro Fontane, Rome, cloister, 1634–7 (C.I.A.)
44. Borromini: S. Carlo alle Quattro Fontane, Rome, cloister, detail (T. Benton)
45. Borromini: Plan for S. Carlo alle Quattro Fontane, Rome, drawing. *Albertina, Vienna, 171* (C.I.A.)
46. S. Carlo alle Quattro Fontane, Rome, drawing shown on illustration 45 with Borromini's second scheme strengthened
47. Borromini: Plan for S. Carlo alle Quattro Fontane, Rome, drawing. *Albertina, Vienna, 173* (C.I.A.)
48. Borromini: Half plan for the church of S. Carlo alle Quattro Fontane, Rome, drawing. *Albertina, Vienna, 175* (Museum photo)
49. Borromini: S. Carlo alle Quattro Fontane, Rome, Lower Church, 1637–41 Portoghesi
50. Borromini: S. Carlo alle Quattro Fontane, Rome, chapel in Lower Church Portoghesi
51. Borromini: S. Carlo alle Quattro Fontane, Rome, interior, 1637–41 (Alinari)
52. Borromini: S. Carlo alle Quattro Fontane, Rome, dome (C.I.A.)
53. Francesco da Volterra: S. Giacomo degli Incurabili, Rome, plan, *c.* 1590
54. Borromini: S. Carlo alle Quattro Fontane, Rome, grille of side-chapel (C.I.A.)
55a and b. Borromini: S. Carlo alle Quattro Fontane, Rome, interior, capitals (C.I.A.)
56a and b. Borromini: S. Carlo alle Quattro Fontane, Rome, niches (C.I.A.)
57. Borromini: S. Carlo alle Quattro Fontane, Rome, façade (Alinari)
58. Borromini: S. Carlo alle Quattro Fontane, Rome, design for façade and towers, drawing. *Albertina, Vienna, 186* (Museum photo)
59. Borromini: S. Carlo alle Quattro Fontane, Rome, drawing for façade. *Albertina, Vienna, 187* (C.I.A.)
60. Borromini: S. Carlo alle Quattro Fontane, Rome, niche on façade

96. Borromini: Design for S. Giovanni in Laterano, Rome, drawing. *Vatican Library, Cod. Vat. Lat. 11258* (C.I.A.)
97. Borromini: Design for S. Giovanni in Laterano, Rome, drawing. *Vatican Library, Cod. Vat. Lat. 11258* (C.I.A.)
98. Borromini: S. Giovanni in Laterano, Rome, entrance wall (C.I.A.)
99. Borromini: S. Giovanni in Laterano, Rome, inner aisle (C.I.A.)
100. Borromini: S. Giovanni in Laterano, Rome, outer aisle (C.I.A.)
101. Borromini: S. Giovanni in Laterano, Rome, base of pilaster in nave (C.I.A.)
102. Borromini: S. Giovanni in Laterano, Rome, base of pilaster in aisle (C.I.A.)
103. Borromini: S. Giovanni in Laterano, Rome, base of statue of St John (C.I.A.)
104. Borromini: S. Giovanni in Laterano, Rome, rail of chapel (C.I.A.)
105. Borromini: S. Giovanni in Laterano, Rome, detail of outer aisle (C.I.A.)
106. Borromini: S. Giovanni in Laterano, Rome, laurel-leaves on pilasters of arches (C.I.A.)
107. Borromini: S. Giovanni in Laterano, Rome, palm-leaves on pilasters of arches (C.I.A.)
108. Borromini: S. Giovanni in Laterano, Rome, tomb of Cardinal de Chaves, after 1655 (C.I.A.)
109. Borromini: S. Giovanni in Laterano, Rome, tomb of Cardinal Giussano, after 1655 (C.I.A.)
110. Borromini: S. Giovanni in Laterano, Rome, tomb of Pope Boniface VIII, after 1655 (C.I.A.)
111. Borromini: S. Giovanni in Laterano, Rome, tomb of Pope Sergius IV, after 1655 (C.I.A.)
112. Borromini: S. Giovanni in Laterano, Rome, tomb of Pope Alexander III, after 1655 (C.I.A.)
113. Borromini: S. Giovanni in Laterano, Rome, baptistery, tomb of Cardinal Ceva, 1650 (C.I.A.)
114. S. Agnese in Piazza Navona, Rome, façade (C.I.A.)
115. S. Agnese in Piazza Navona, Rome, interior (Anderson)
116. Borromini: Façade of S. Agnese in Piazza Navona, Rome, drawing. *Albertina, Vienna, 59a* (Museum photo)
117. Borromini: Design for Palazzo Carpegna, Rome, drawing. *Albertina, Vienna, 1017a* (Museum photo)
118. Borromini: Design for Palazzo Carpegna, Rome, drawing. *Albertina, Vienna, 1014a* (Museum photo)
119. Borromini: Design for Palazzo Carpegna, Rome, drawing. *Albertina, Vienna, 1015* (Museum photo)
120. Borromini: Design for Palazzo Carpegna, Rome, drawing. *Albertina, Vienna, 1019b* (Museum photo)
121. Borromini: Design for Palazzo Carpegna, Rome, drawing. *Albertina, Vienna, 1018* (Museum photo)
122. Borromini: Palazzo Carpegna, Rome, arch between loggia and staircase, after 1643 (C.I.A.)
123. Borromini: Design for first floor of Palazzo Carpegna, Rome, drawing. *Albertina, Vienna, 1010* (Museum photo)
124. Borromini: Palazzo Falconieri, Rome, pilaster on street front, after 1645 (Dr P. Cannon Brookes)
125. Borromini: Palazzo Falconieri, Rome, front towards the Tiber (Anderson)
126. Borromini: Palazzo Falconieri, Rome, ceiling (C.I.A.)
127. Borromini: Palazzo Pamphili, Rome, ceiling of *salone* (C.I.A.)
128. Palazzo Pamphili, Rome, gallery, after 1647 (C.I.A.)
129. Borromini: Casino del Bufalo, Rome, door, engraving (From Rossi, *Studio d'architettura civile*, 1702–21)

# Index